Michael Wood

FILM

A Very Short Introduction

OXFORD
UNIVERSITY PRESS

OXFORD
UNIVERSITY PRESS

Great Clarendon Street, Oxford ox2 6DP

Oxford University Press is a department of the University of Oxford.
It furthers the University's objective of excellence in research, scholarship,
and education by publishing worldwide in

Oxford New York

Auckland Cape Town Dar es Salaam Hong Kong Karachi
Kuala Lumpur Madrid Melbourne Mexico City Nairobi
New Delhi Shanghai Taipei Toronto

With offices in

Argentina Austria Brazil Chile Czech Republic France Greece
Guatemala Hungary Italy Japan Poland Portugal Singapore
South Korea Switzerland Thailand Turkey Ukraine Vietnam

Oxford is a registered trade mark of Oxford University Press
in the UK and in certain other countries

Published in the United States
by Oxford University Press Inc., New York

© Michael Wood 2012

The moral rights of the author have been asserted
Database right Oxford University Press (maker)

First published 2012

British Library Cataloguing in Publication Data

Data available

Library of Congress Cataloging in Publication Data

Data available

Typeset by SPI Publisher Services, Pondicherry, India
Printed in Great Britain
on acid-free paper by
Ashford Colour Press Ltd, Gosport, Hampshire

ISBN 978-0-19-280353-5

1 3 5 7 9 10 8 6 4 2

Available soon:

For more information visit our website

www.oup.com/vsi/

Contents

List of illustrations

Publisher's acknowledgements

'The Poetry of Departures' taken from *Collected Poems* (2004) © Philip Larkin and reproduced by permission of Faber and Faber Ltd (UK and rest of world rights).

Excerpts from "Poetry of Departures" from COLLECTED POEMS by Philip Larkin. Copyright © 1988, 2003 by the Estate of Philip Larkin. Reprinted by permission of Farrar, Straus and Giroux, LLC (US rights).

Before the titles

I should like to apologize for two kinds of absence from this book. First, that of all the films, directors, writers, stories, thoughts, facts I have loved and couldn't find a place for – because I was too busy finding a place for something else. The pragmatic justification for such an exclusion, of course, is that life is short and so are very short introductions. But pragmatism doesn't exclude a little sadness.

I have taken my examples chiefly from Europe, North America, and Japan. This is because these places are the homes of the films I know best and have lived with longest, and the advantage of this approach is a certain security of description and consistency of thought. But since there is scarcely a country in the world where films have not been made, the limitations of this strategy are obvious, and create the second, larger absence I have in mind. Or part of it, since there are also plenty of European, North American, and Japanese works I haven't seen. This absence is that of all the films, directors, writers, stories, thoughts, facts, and doubtless many other ingredients that I don't know or didn't think of. Some of these elements are probably crucial and would have altered my whole view of film if I had been able to take them into account. I miss them on principle. But as one of the themes of this book suggests, you can know what you can't see but you can't see what you don't know.

Of course, it is impossible to survey or summarize the world of film, and I have not tried. But I hope it is possible to open up questions about what has been happening to the medium and through the medium, about what it is like to have learned to take for granted what once seemed to be a miracle: images of life possessing the movement of life itself. We must be seeing things.

Chapter 1
Moving pictures

Still waters

A man stands before a grave in a country cemetery. He doesn't move, nothing moves; no birds, a still world. But this is a man in a motion picture, we have seen him move, and he will move again in a moment when his spell of meditation and memory is over. The film is John Ford's *Young Mr Lincoln* (1939). The man is Henry Fonda playing a grieving Lincoln as he lingers over Ann Rutledge's grave.

You like the shot and its framing, so you pause the film. Now it looks and feels quite different. How can it? What could be the difference between a stilled and a moving picture of a scene where there is no movement? You start the film again, and pause it again. Yes, quite different. Then you realize. There is a river at the back of the image, and in the motion picture it flows, there are pieces of ice drifting down the dark surface. In the still, it doesn't even look like a river, it looks like a piece of cloth, you would know it was a river only by induction.

For a long time, film studios all over the world were in the habit of advertising their wares not through actual images from their movies, but by means of publicity photographs: still pictures of stationary actors, often posed to look as if they were in a scene

1. Still waters

from a film, but also often posed for scenes that didn't appear in any film at all. Large posters for movies didn't display photographs but lurid graphic representations, high-colour, lavishly stylized images from the world of commercial painting. Both practices suggested that a piece of a film couldn't announce a film in an adequate way, as indeed it couldn't, and can't. A stopped frame of a movie isn't part of the movie, unless the movie is using this frame as part of its design. A stopped frame outside of a movie isn't anything, not even a photograph. If nothing else moves in *Young Mr Lincoln*, the water in the river does; and if the water doesn't move, it isn't a movie.

And yet it doesn't move, as Galileo didn't quite say. A film is made up of precisely those stills that aren't anything – that aren't anything until they are projected at the right speed, 24 frames a second (or once upon a time, 18 frames). Then we see the real river not behind the simulated Abraham Lincoln but behind the real Henry Fonda. There's more. We not only see movement where there is none, we fail to see, or our brains skilfully occlude from us, the swift patches of darkness between the frames. 'This temporal continuity', Mary Ann Doane says, referring to so-called 'real time' on screen, 'is in fact haunted by absence, by the lost time represented by the division between frames. During the projection of a film, the spectator is sitting in an unperceived darkness for almost 40 percent of the running time.'

I'm not sure the experience of light and motion is really haunted by any absence at all for most viewers of most films. We see what we see: motion. The effect became fully available to us only in 1895, soon after we learned how to get horseless carriages to move by means of an internal combustion engine, and shortly before we learned how to get aeroplanes to stay in the air. Still, it's intriguing to recall the actual make-up of what we are seeing when we see a movie. It's worth remembering too that all perception of movement, even that of the real world, is illusory as regards continuity. The brain constantly receives and makes sense of stimuli, combines them into what look like pictures of a steadily moving or stationary world. Reality is recorded by the eyes, so to speak, and composed by the brain. 'Each eye movement gives the retina a "snapshot" of some part of the visual scene, but the brain must put these still pictures together to create the illusion of a continuous world. Even neuroscientists don't have much of an idea about how this complicated process works.' Where there is movement, the brain doesn't watch a movie, it makes a movie; it is producer and director and movie theatre all in one.

Moving pictures both capture and make motion, and they do it by means of the magic I've just described: a mixture of speed and light. This magic remains magic even if we understand how it works and call it technology. What is still remains still and also moves. But then we have to remind ourselves that what we are seeing is not an illusion in the most frequently used sense of the term: 'Something that deceives or deludes by producing a false

2. Light in the dark

impression' (*Oxford English Dictionary*). The impression produced by a film may be exactly the opposite of false. We really see the movement, and the movement is often real. If we had been at a railway station in France on a famous cinematic occasion, we would have seen the train too, the camera didn't make it up. And what we see now on the screen when we watch that piece of early film – the Lumière Brothers' *Arrivée d'un train en gare de La Ciotat* (1895) – is not just technology. It is the result of a technology that allows us to supply the missing movement and to miss the too-swift passage of the empty spaces. What haunts us, if anything haunts us, is knowledge of a state of affairs not a rival vision – the invisible reality haunts the world of the visible and often infinitely plausible ghosts. 'Who you gonna believe, me or your own eyes?' This is Chico Marx's question to Margaret Dumont in *Duck Soup* (1933), and a great moment in early film theory. I'll return to it later in this chapter. We have to believe our own eyes, we don't really have a choice. But sometimes we have to believe other agencies as well.

4

There is something both tantalizing and incoherent about the idea of unperceived darkness and of a movement that both does and does not exist; and there's an interesting philosophical slippage on this subject in a well-known article by Joseph and Barbara Anderson, in which movement in film is presented both as real and not real. 'To the visual system', they write, 'the motion in a motion picture is real motion.' And then: 'We know that the individual pictures of a motion picture are not really moving, and that our perception of motion is therefore an illusion.' We see one thing and we know another, but we can talk about this fact, it seems, only by contradicting ourselves. It's not that the movement of the image seems real but is an illusion. It is real as far as our immediate perceptual system is concerned; it just breaks down under analysis into still frames. A matter, so to speak, of different speeds of looking.

What is a film? What is film? If you have picked up this book, even to glance at it, you will have certain meanings in mind and not others. You probably are not thinking, for example, of cataracts on the eyes or, more generally, in the words of *Webster's Dictionary*, of 'a thin skin', a 'haze' or 'mist', or the transparent wrapping material that in England is called 'cling film'. A very short introduction to any of these things might make a fine book, but it almost certainly isn't what you're expecting. Nor are you thinking most immediately, I would guess, of what another dictionary calls 'an extremely thin pellicle or lamina of any material', although one form of such a lamina, the strip of coated material which receives and stores moving images, does get us closer to our goal.

A film is a roll of such material that can be run through a projector in order to throw moving images, or images of movement, on a screen. And it is also, of course, a name for what is projected on the screen as well as the art and industry of making such images. It is in this sense that we understand the word in phrases like 'film star' or 'film fan' or 'film critic' – although the sense here, broad in one aspect, is narrow in another. Film stars don't usually act in

documentary films or home movies, and fans love to confuse
actors with their fictional roles. A film, when not otherwise
specified, is often taken to be a feature film of a certain length,
telling a detailed story of imaginary people, the movie cousin of a
play or a novel, and offered for public consumption. Scholars tell
us that statistically such works do not form anywhere near a
majority of the films that have been made or are being made; but
the usage is still in place and perfectly intelligible.

Here are two of the *Oxford English Dictionary*'s definitions:

> A cinematographic representation of a story, drama, episode, event,
> etc.; a cinema performance; pl. the cinema, the 'pictures', the
> movies.

> Film-making considered as an art-form.

I would want to amplify the notion of film-making, and its attendant
activity of film-watching. Taken together, these practices constitute
something more than an art-form, and something more than a
variety of entertainment. Let's call it for the moment an institution:
an enterprise and a cultural ritual all rolled, or reeled, into one.

And I shall have one further sense of film in mind throughout the
book: film as footage, a set of images of movement of any kind,
actual or imaginary, short or long, produced by anyone or any film
technology whatsoever – that is, even when the spatial dimension
of the term 'footage' has vanished. This is not my main subject,
which is film in its chief or basic usage, but I'd like the reader to
think the term *always* means footage, whatever else it may also
richly mean. As Hollis Frampton says, 'Films are made out of
footage, not out of the world at large.' A film in this acceptation
simply stores and shows movement, and is treasured (or hated or
banned) for this reason if for no other. The films of the Lumière
Brothers meet this criterion, of course, and so do the films of

Georges Meliès; between them, they begin to define it. But so do newsreels, every feature film ever made, all documentary films, all art installations involving film, all visual records of surveillance, all music videos, all clips of film shown on television, all television programmes not broadcast live, every amateur moving picture of baby's first smile, and all glimpses of political demonstrations or riots taken on mobile phones and emailed to the world. Such footage pictures the past, whether very old or very recent, as still alive and in motion. It pictures a time and a place not (usually) immediately accessible to the viewer but often unbearably real in the effect their contents create. Our relation to film as footage is a part of our relation to film as film.

Most of us have surely at some point been bowled over by the movement of images on a screen. Even what seem fairly crude old devices can still catch us out. I remember seeing D. W. Griffiths' film *Way Down East* (1920) some time in the 1980s. The showing was in a New York movie theatre, and the crowd was mildly giggling for much of the time. It's true that most of the movie felt like a hokey melodrama from another planet – the mid-19th-century stage, for example. Then as Lillian Gish got herself stranded on an ice floe heading straight for a vast waterfall, everyone fell silent. And when her rescue was effected at what seemed to be later than the last possible minute, the previously scornful person behind me muttered 'Christ Almighty' in audible relief.

Nothing ever dies on film – even corpses are mobile, visibly carried around in their coffins or tracked from more than one angle. Virginia Woolf said long ago that on film 'We see life as it is when we have no part in it'. Of course, we don't exactly see life as it is, but what we see certainly seems to be living, it feels much more vivid than any representation could – and indeed, it is not exactly a representation, it is a trace. This is why our having no part in it seems so strange, almost impossible.

These very terms, film and footage, are approaching obsolescence in their material meaning, and I have already misused them in relation to mobile phones. There is no reel in a digital camera, and nothing there that can be measured in length. In their larger meaning, though, I think it's unlikely that the terms will disappear. And if they do, we shall find other names for what they used to name: arranged sets of moving images, and sequences of moving images that may scarcely be arranged at all. The difference between stock and footage – or between whatever elements they correspond to in the future – is helpful in this respect. Stock is film (in the material sense) that films (as projectable objects) are shot on. Footage is film we can watch.

Film and photography

Of course, film is photography, or a form of it. The common technological origin is important, and is the source of much of the authority and allure of film as a medium. Or to be truly precise, the set of ideas we have built around that origin is the source of this authority and allure.

These ideas all involve the notion that a photograph will inevitably reveal something about reality, as if every scene could be read like a crime scene. Walter Benjamin tells us that when looking at a photograph, 'the beholder feels an irresistible urge to search ... for the tiny spark of contingency ... with which reality has so to speak seared the subject'. We have an 'unruly desire' to know about the persons in a photograph, about the actual life they had before and after the photographer got to them. The camera bypasses the notion of art, even when it aims at art, and reveals to us what Benjamin calls the 'optical unconscious'. He means all the details stopped motion can show us – Muybridge's demonstration that a running horse at one point has all four feet off the ground – and also the minutiae of facial expression that no one could intend to show or find, the early wrinkle, the faint grimace, the fear behind the eyes, 'physiognomic aspects of visual worlds which dwell in the smallest things, meaningful yet covert enough to find a hiding place in waking dreams'. 'Photography is pure contingency and can be nothing else', Roland Barthes says. 'It is as if the photograph always carries its referent with itself.' It is 'a chemical revelation'. Stanley Cavell reminds us that a film is always a film of something: even if the scenery is fake, it's real fake scenery. The suggestion is not that the camera cannot lie, but that it cannot close its eyes. 'Photography and the cinema', André Bazin says, 'are discoveries that satisfy, once and for all and in its very essence, our obsession with realism'.

This is all very emphatic, and may seem mildly deluded, or displaced. Photographs can't guarantee the reality of what they show just because they are traced in light by a machine rather than drawn in ink or paint by a human hand. It's true that the camera can catch contingency as no other instrument can. Not true that everything it catches is contingency – think of all the spontaneously photographed moments that turn out to have been elaborately set up in advance. Nor is it true that a photograph always carries its referent with it, only that it may. The referent can be faked: I have a photograph of Queen Victoria taking tea with President McKinley, whom she never met. Benjamin is right to suggest that cameras often see what we can't see – that's why the looks on the faces of our relatives in old snapshots are so revealing and (sometimes) so touching – but the interest of the reminder that a photograph is always a photograph of something is very slender. Of course, we wouldn't have a photo of Queen Victoria if she hadn't existed, but we wouldn't have any paintings either, and I'm not sure how much a photo of a real waxwork Queen Victoria would tell us about anything except waxworks. And finally, it can't be right to say that photography and the cinema have satisfied our obsession with realism, if we have one, because nothing will.

If I see photographs (digital or analogue) of my friends or family, I recognize them at once, and if I see them in a particular place,

I take the photograph as evidence that they were there. Similarly, if my image is caught on a surveillance machine as I am robbing a bank, I shall not expect the judge to have any sympathy with a defence based on the history of photography. In fact, what Benjamin and Barthes are describing to us, and what Cavell and Bazin are relying a touch too heavily upon, is not the actual or original relation of photography to the world but our intense and unmistakable feeling about that relation. I don't think any of these writers are deceiving themselves about their focus, but they allow themselves to be read as if they were. Bazin, for example, writes of 'the irrational power of photography, in which we believe without reservation' – a cultural belief, even one without reservation, is not the same as the acceptance of an unavoidable fact, but we might not make the distinction immediately. The power and the belief could arise from what we know of the technology – from the fact that photographs trace the world rather than represent it – but in many, perhaps most, cases, it must come from the extraordinary strength of resemblance we find in the image.

The effect of reality in photographs is about as real as effects can get, the best such effect human beings have ever achieved. This is what Bazin must mean by the obsession with realism – the obsession is not with the real but with reproductions of the real, what Aristotle used to call 'mimesis'. One of the most curious of many curious questions in the supposedly transparent *Poetics* is that of our delight in imitation, a primary instinct, Aristotle thought, and a universal pleasure.

> We have evidence of this in the facts of experience. Objects which in themselves we view with pain, we delight to contemplate when reproduced with minute fidelity: such as the forms of ignoble animals and dead bodies.

How Aristotle would have loved the movies, especially horror movies! It's true that he catches himself up quickly and tells us that the point of all this is that we like to learn things, but the flicker of pure unimproving pleasure is unmistakable. Our hankering for ever more meticulous copying of the real does indeed seem to be unstoppable, and it must come from a pleasure in simulation itself.

This pleasure and these questions are beautifully played out in a very early (1908) film version of *The Tempest*. The director is Percy Stow (1876–1919), who shot more than 250 short films between 1901 and 1916. Prospero is over-made-up and over-acting, and setting off fireworks in a manifestly cardboard cave. The argument that the camera always catches the referent doesn't do anything for us here, or not yet. We just wish we were not seeing so much real cardboard. But then through the cardboard, we catch sight of the sea. The real sea. That is, the photographed real sea, or at least photographed real water (the scene is no doubt shot in a studio tank). Dark waves curl in towards us, foam at their tops, a piece of the natural world in motion as convincing as we are ever likely to glimpse, and all the more startling because we glimpse it through the real cardboard that is fake rock. What is happening here?

First, although the sea appears to be as real as it can be, we are not confused. We know this is a moving picture, and we are not afraid of getting wet, as the first spectators of the Lumières' train were said to be afraid of getting run over. Second, we do not, and I suggest cannot, think that this pictured sea is really a series of still photographs projected at a certain speed. That's not what we're seeing. It is only an image, but it is a moving image of moving matter. If we've seen the sea, we say that's it, and if we have never seen the sea, then, as Aristotle suggests for a similar case, 'the pleasure will be due not to the imitation as such, but to the execution…or some such other cause'. No, it won't, it will be due to our seeing on screen what looks like the sheer reality of the sea we don't know, and if even Aristotle is willing to abandon his whole argument about imitation in this extraordinarily cavalier way ('some such other cause'), we know we must be in very interesting and difficult conceptual country.

3. Real fakery

Who you gonna believe?

This is the moment to return to what I called the instance of early film theory in *Duck Soup*, a film we know must be dangerous because Mussolini took the trouble to ban it. The wonderfully improbable plot of the film hinges on the stealing of some plans kept in a safe to which Margaret Dumont has the code. The Italian-accented Chico has locked the ever wise-cracking Groucho in a cupboard in his bedroom and we hear the prisoner complaining, banging on the door ('Let me out of here, or throw me a magazine', 'I'll see my lawyer about this as soon as he graduates from law school'); see Chico disguise himself as Groucho (long white nightshirt, nightcap, moustache, glasses, cigar) and trot towards Margaret Dumont's room. She's not surprised to see him, but she is surprised by his accent and asks him why he is talking like that. He says he may go to Italy one day so he is practising. She turns away to look for the code for the safe, and the silent Harpo enters the room, also disguised as Groucho – as with Chico, we have seen him put on the complete outfit. Chico dives under the bed. Margaret Dumont hands over to Harpo a slip of paper with the code and continues the conversation. Harpo makes all kinds of Groucho faces, but doesn't (obviously, since he is the silent Harpo) speak. He quacks the horn he has under his nightshirt, and Margaret Dumont, thinking he sounds a little hoarse, wonders whether he would like a drink of water. She turns away, and Harpo glimpses Chico under the bed. Harpo swiftly exits as Margaret Dumont turns with the water. She begins to take off her dressing gown, and then is shocked to realize that Chico, whom we have seen emerge from his hiding place, is still in the room. Didn't she just see him leave? He says not, and she says, 'But I saw you with my own eyes'. He says, 'Well, who you gonna believe, me or your own eyes?'

It's a rhetorical question for him, and of course, in one sense, he's right. He hasn't left the room. And he knows as well as anyone that she's not doing too well by believing her own eyes. She has taken both him and Harpo for Groucho. She's done slightly better by believing her ears, since she picked up Chico's accent at once; but then lapsed immediately by believing him, or what he implausibly says. And then she lapsed further aurally by not hearing Harpo's silence as anything other than silence, and by failing to distinguish between the honk of a tooted horn and the sound of a cough.

And yet. Chico's statement that he didn't leave, although true, is incomplete. He was hiding under the bed, and had left her sight. Otherwise, she couldn't have thought she saw him leave – that is, actually have seen Harpo leave and thought it was Chico whom she had taken for Groucho. More important, her eyes are not deceiving her, the brothers' disguises are. There is also something very strange about the completeness of the visual resemblance. It's

13

as if there is only one brother, or as if all it takes to be Groucho Marx is a kit: moustache, cigar, glasses, nightshirt, nightcap – with a touch of the walk thrown in. In this sense, perhaps even Groucho is an impersonation of Groucho.

We know there are three Grouchos because we have seen two of them don the disguise; but then we are believing our own eyes. In this case, our eyes tell us about the disguise even as they accept the resemblance once the disguise is on. Margaret Dumont lacks this information, and although we laugh at her gullibility, we might pause for a moment to wonder what sort of world we would have to be in to suspect that the prime minister even of this absurd country has a double, or even two. A Marx Brothers movie, perhaps, but it's an essential part of the joke that she can't suspect that; and that the Brothers should seem never to have lived anywhere else. It's true that perhaps only a person trapped inside a Marx Brothers movie could fail to distinguish, as we so readily distinguish, Groucho's fast New York slang from Chico's exaggerated Italian accent and both of them from Harpo's silence.

So whom should Margaret Dumont believe? Her eyes are right but she draws the wrong inference from their input. And yet she can't believe the person in front of her instead because the truth he is telling is only a fraction of a larger lie: he is not the person he is supposed to be.

And whom or what are we going to believe? Everyone and everything, surely. We can't unsee what we have seen, not have heard what we have heard. The question is what else we are going to do. All movies rely on visual evidence to an extraordinary degree. By 'rely on', I mean put to use in ways that are characteristic of the medium. Sometimes the evidence will seem irrefutable, this is how documentaries and newsreels are supposed to work, offering us, in Patricia Aufderheide's helpful phrase, 'a pledge…that what we will see and hear is about something real and true'. Admittedly, a pledge is not a proof, but nothing's perfect.

Often, the visual evidence will convince us once we have made a series of supplementary connections – we put together the implied historical or fictional world and are content with the result. Sometimes, as so often in Hitchcock, the apparent evidence will simply lie to us. Our eyes, if we are watching *North by Northwest* (1959), show us a man holding a dead man in his arms and a knife in his hand. Anyone would think the man who's alive has killed the man who is dead, and pretty much everyone in the film does. Whom are we going to believe? Cary Grant or our own eyes? Very often, when the medium of film is up to its most interesting work, a tense dialogue between what we see/hear and what we believe will structure the whole work, placing a strong emphasis on the sheer temptation to believe our eyes and ears – a temptation that I take to be essential to the medium, that is stronger in the cinema than it can be anywhere outside.

We know without a doubt that we can't tell just by looking at it whether a glass of milk is poisoned, but it is part of the magic and the insidious psychology of Hitchcock's *Suspicion* (1941) that we find ourselves almost believing that looking will do the trick. This is why we stare and stare at the glass on the tray as Cary Grant, that specialist in dubious appearances, takes it up to Joan Fontaine's bedroom. Or rather, our own strange compulsion, let's call it a prejudice in favour of the visual, as if it were a friend or a relative we wish could perform far better than they can, is compounded by Hitchcock's intimate awareness of our compulsion, and by his having placed a light bulb inside the milk, creating a glow which seems like a promise of crucial knowledge.

It's an important aspect of these games with vision, these worries and adventures in the realms of knowing, that we don't ordinarily say, in any idiomatic way, that we do believe our own eyes. We say only that we can't believe them, and even then we don't mean we think we are not seeing what we are seeing. We do the same when we say 'This isn't happening to me'. We say it because it is; and because we wish it wasn't. What all this suggests is that in certain circumstances – circumstances that film in particular creates and exploits – seeing can't be controverted, only contextualized, complemented by other stories.

Fast history

This book is not a history of film, even a speeded-up one, but it is good to know where we are in time. It could all have been different. What if we had learned how to record moving images but not how to project them; or could project them for only one person at a time, never progressing beyond a more and more sophisticated peepshow? What if we had learned how to project them to any number of people but the amusement had never caught on beyond the fairground or the variety show? Or if we had decided to project films only for scientific or artistic reasons, never for sheer entertainment? If the projection device had worked in the home but not for a larger public – that is, if some form of television had preceded cinema?

I mention these possibilities not to propose alternative histories but to suggest how particular and contingent any actual history is. This is in part why the long prehistory of film is so absorbing. Since very ancient times – there were experiments in Egypt and Rome around the time of the birth of Christ – people have been interested in making and seeing images of movement, and by the 19th century the world was full of inventions with names that themselves sound like a cabinet of wonders: Zoetrope, Eidophusikon, Tachyscope, Chromatrope, Eidotrope. The studies of motion by Étienne-Jules Marey and Eadweard Muybridge are especially important and fascinating – there is something truly dizzying in the thought that an extreme expertise in stopping motion was an essential prelude to starting plausible pictures of it. Even now, one has only to riffle the pages of an old flicker book (or a contemporary flicker book made for children) to get a feeling for the early days of film. In 1987, Arlene Croce wrote a wonderful book on Fred Astaire and Ginger Rogers that had small photographic frames at the top corners of the right-hand pages. You flicked the pages and saw the famous couple dance. Many of the stills in the book gave us a better sense of what they actually looked like, but the flickering frames enacted for us, however awkwardly, the exact feeling of a musical number in a movie.

Still, the essential elements come clearly together only on a day in December 1895, when Auguste and Louis Lumière made the first public display of what their Cinematograph could do, namely project as a film what had been filmed... on film. Actually, the first film to be screened for a paying audience was a four-minute sequence of two boxers going at it in Madison Square Garden – this had happened in May of the same year – but the Lumière show was considerably more developed. They exhibited ten works, and it's worth pausing briefly over a couple of them, and especially over the first and most famous.

This is called *La Sortie de l'usine Lumière à Lyon*, usually known in English just as *Leaving the Factory*. The gates of a workplace open and a crowd of workers, mainly women, comes out, walking first towards the stationary camera and then veering right or left. More precisely, since there is already a good deal of composition in this apparently primitive picture, the women cross in waves as they come towards us, those starting on the right moving to the left, and vice versa. The large drift seems as certain as that of the sea, or a river. But there are exceptions. Not everyone in the crowd follows this dominant pattern. A couple of men with bicycles seem to be going entirely their own way, and a dog wanders in and out of the foreground. The effect is amazing. At first glance, there is a disorderly mass, a sheer profusion of people. At second glance, profusion yields to pattern, and you don't know whether to believe that contingency itself has an order – people do leave factories according to habits of movement – or that the camera has imposed its order upon the world. It all seems rather jerky and old now, but it must once have seemed immensely real – real people leaving a real factory, real dogs and bikes. There could be no denying what any of them were, and no one had ever seen a representation of reality as real as this except in a photograph, and these people were moving. It wasn't a representation, of course, any more than a photograph was. It was a trace, the gathering of a residue left in light, like a shadow or a fingerprint. But then reality itself, whether caught in the act or created in the camera, turned out to offer an extraordinary combination of pattern and randomness, of waves and dogs.

L'arroseur arrosé is rather different, a short comic set piece. It doesn't have the impact of the workers leaving the factory, in part because nothing can quite have the impact of that first (actual or belatedly imagined) encounter with what looks like a bit of undeniable reality on the move, and in part because the whole thing feels like a set-up, and the very title ('the waterer watered') announces some sort of fable. A man stands in a large walled garden, peacefully using a hose pipe on his plants. A boy tiptoes up behind him, puts his foot on the pipe, stopping the flow of water. The gardener bends over his hose, staring at it as if an inspection of the thing could tell him what the problem is. The boy takes his foot off the pipe and the gardener gets a sudden faceful of water. He chases the boy, catches him, and gives him a (not very convincing) spanking, and sends him out of the frame. The gardener returns to his initial posture, water flows, and the garden is again calm. There's no moral to this sequence that I can see, but there is a shape and an irony. There is a story, in other words, as there is not in the exit from the factory.

Taken together, these films sketch out a good deal of what moving pictures will be. They will catch (or hope or pretend to catch) the real as it looks when nothing is happening, when there is no story – or to put that another way, when what is happening is only what happens every day. And they will pick specific moments, wait for the instances when something quite out of the ordinary occurs, a joke, a death, an infidelity, a historical event. We could think of surveillance cameras as fulfilling precisely these two functions. They need to watch over and record all the empty time when no one is robbing anyone, so that they can be there on cue when someone is. A camera that switched on only when a crime was taking place would be an eerie invention, a sort of oracle rather than recorder of reality. But a camera that watched only the ordinary would seem a little strange too – this is the strangeness sought by films like Andy Warhol's *Sleep* (1963), or his *Empire* (1964) – since it is our belief (our superstition) that even the ordinary is redeemed now and then by an event. We could think of films as placed along a spectrum from a place where (almost) nothing happens to a region where there is (almost) nothing but one manic event after the other. The difference would lie not in reality but in whether the film-maker is intrigued by the uneventful or anxious to banish it: Erich von Stroheim at one end, the Marx Brothers at the other. Or to take later examples, Douglas Gordon's 24-hour version of Hitchcock's *Psycho* and any Hong Kong action movie.

So with the Cinematograph, do we have cinema, film as we know it? Not quite. The Lumière Brothers didn't think their invention had any commercial value, although they thought it might help science, and even the prodigiously inventive Georges Meliès didn't at first think that films would go beyond being fancy acts within a larger, live show. It took Thomas Edison to see what now seems obvious to us: there was gold in them there stills – once they looked as if they moved. Charles Musser tells us that in April 1896, Edison's Vitascope machine was showing films in one venue in the United States. A year later, there were several hundred projectors across the country and as far as Honolulu. With Edison, film became a business, and although it took some time for the medium to get beyond the nickelodeon stage, those early cinemas where 5 cents would allow you to see a whole set of short films, the road was clear, and a lot of people were soon on it. Large numbers of films began to be made in France, England, Italy, the USA, and people flocked to see them.

With this shift, the invention of film was in one sense complete. In another sense, it hadn't even begun. The language of film as we know it had yet to be born. The history of this language is fascinating, and I can't even scratch at it here, much less sort out the credits, how much and what is owed to Edwin Porter and others, and how much of the language was in place before D. W. Griffith made it feel like an articulated system. It will be enough for our present purposes to say what had to happen.

The camera had to learn to move: to close in, to back away, to track laterally, to perch on a crane, even, later, to do several of these things in one take. André Bazin made what he saw as a crucial distinction between fast cutting from shot to shot in film and the possibilities of deep focus, between the construction of meaning in the editing and the discovery of meaning in the image. But it may be that a more practical, immediate distinction is that between editing in the cutting room and editing in the camera, through the selective, unbroken movements of the machine. To get a sense of how elaborate (and how beautiful) this formal invention can be, you might first take a look at any old film where the camera doesn't move, but just sits and snaps whatever comes towards it or crosses its view, and then follow the camera's acrobatics in the long opening single take of Orson Welles' *Touch of Evil* (1958). We see, in close-up, a bomb being placed in the boot of a car, then we climb away backwards over a set of buildings, drop down into the next street, where a couple is walking towards a border patrol – we are on the frontier between Mexico and the USA. We watch various border crossings, see new arrivals at the checkpoint. The couple, having crossed into Mexico, stop and kiss, and as they do the bomb explodes, six and a half minutes after the take started.

If you don't have the Welles movie to hand, you might enjoy the opening scene of Robert Altman's *The Player* (1992), where the Welles take is discussed and amiably parodied, as the camera peers through the window of a movie studio office, follows people out of a building, shifts in and out of close-up and long shot, watches the arrival of cars and tourists, and returns to the office, all without a break, and with a quiet touch of the Latin beat of Welles' soundtrack in the music by Thomas Newman. Altman's take is quite a bit longer than six and a half minutes. The story in Welles and Altman could well have been told in a series of separate shots; but our sense of the teller and how he saw the world would have been different. For another striking instance of a camera movement telling us something, we could look at the high-angle shot in *Family Plot* (1976), where Hitchcock, not ordinarily much given to fancy camera work, tracks two characters along separate paths in a cemetery, the diverging and converging design of their movements bringing together elements of the story till now separate, as if diagramming a destiny.

But I'm getting a little ahead of myself, or ahead of my fast history. We had to learn how to edit too, once a film went beyond the tale or scene in the single shot. Any juxtaposition of shots in time (and in space, once the use of a split screen becomes possible) creates meaning, the way any two words will make some sort of sense, even if all grammar is lacking. Or rather, we make sense, as we so readily understand the linguist's instance of 'colourless green ideas sleep furiously'. This possibility (this inevitability) is the basis of Eisenstein's theory of montage, which concerns precisely the relation between or among images, and it is the reason why Noel Burch can conclude that 'shot transition' is the basic element of film practice. But most of the time, in film as in language, we do have a grammar to help us, we are not stranded in some kind of everyday surrealism. A shot of a person looking off-screen is followed by a shot of something, anything. That is what the person is looking at, even if it happens to have been photographed in another time and another country. A person speaks, looking to the left. In the next shot, a person listens, looking to the right. This is a conversation, they are in the same room or street or car. Of course, films can and do show people and what they are looking at in the same frame; people talking to each other too. But the separate shots I have described are an essential part of film-making and film-watching, precisely because of the continuous space that is constructed – that is made available by the director's choice of sequence, and made intelligible by our creation of an implied world we can peer into. 'She stops crying to watch some pigeons settle on the spire of a church', Luis Buñuel wrote in an article on Dreyer's *Passion of Joan of Arc*. That is, a shot of her face is followed by a shot of some birds.

The rule of grammar here – a rule Buñuel himself mischievously breaks in *Un Chien andalou* (1929), for example, by having a man leave a room only to find himself arriving in the room he apparently left – is called shot-countershot, and P. Adams Sitney tells us that 'it took some twenty years for this figure of editing to become the cornerstone of a narrative continuity in films. By the end of the First World War, it was a firmly established convention.' But then, no one noticed it much unless someone broke the rule. Or operated by a different rule, that of parallel editing, also known as cross-cutting, which offers the precise opposite of the logic of shot-countershot. Here an image of, say, our heroine tied to the train tracks is followed by an image of her rescuer trying to reach her before the thundering express does. The two figures inhabit the same time but different spaces, until – after the suspense has been sufficiently drawn out – they meet in the same space and she is saved. The point in both cases, whether the space we construct is single or double, is that we shall have made narrative space out of sheer sequence, just as we shall have lent two-dimensional figures the third dimension we are sure they have in their own habitat. The moviegoer works less hard than the reader of books, in one sense, since so much is shown to her, pictured as complete in itself. But she also works harder in another sense, since she has a whole surrounding world to create, and all the syntax is in her head rather than on the screen.

The close-up looks at first as if it belongs to the realm of camera work only, and not that of editing, but in fact it belongs to both.

If there were no long or middle range shots on either side of it, we could not speak of a close-up. And if separate shots prior to montage, as the Russian film-maker and theorist Kuleshov says, constitute not cinema 'but only the material for cinema', we may wish to recall, with the linguist Roman Jakobson, that a close-up turns an image into a sign, loads it with meaning, and incorporates it into a language. There are literary antecedents for these devices. Dickens was a master of the close-up, and Flaubert appears to have invented cross-cutting when in *Madame Bovary* he spliced the announcement of prizes at an agricultural fair with the seduction patter of a country Don Juan. But in literature, the devices remain minor effects. In films, they carry whole stories and arguments along. I recall Marcel Ophuls watching some of his own earlier work, and fretting at what he felt were the too obvious tricks he had been using. 'Look', he would say impatiently, 'there's another close-up on the hands'. He meant there are more subtle ways of suggesting someone is nervous.

There are all kinds of other devices characteristic of the cinema. There are camera movements like zooms and panning, or the sudden bringing into clear focus (known as racking) which in many recent films takes the place of a cut or a close-up, since it also is a way of drawing our attention to a detail or a person. At the level of editing and sequence, there are dissolves, fade-ins, fade-outs, freeze-frames, the use of an iris, slow motion, much more. I mention them for the record and to suggest something of the richness of the resources at a film-maker's disposal; and also more tendentiously to suggest that once these elements are available to a director, and easily readable by an audience, film has reached its maturity as a medium and an art-form. There are no more changes to come.

No? What about sound and colour? Computer-generated imagery? The whole digital revolution? We'll come to the revolution later in this book, but I'm suggesting that sound and colour have not altered the basic idioms of film in any serious way, however much they have altered its reach and looks and increased its affective power. This is true in principle even of techniques like voice-over narrative or commentary, which have been used in both brilliant and boring ways, but can be thought of (contentiously) as modernized title-cards.

Film literacy, so to speak, has remained pretty much what it was soon after people had stopped regretting the end of silence. Of course, all kinds of things have happened to alter the 'classical perfection' André Bazin dated to 1938 or 1939, and many styles and anti-styles have arisen. Many new topics too. But a person who understood the language of film in 1939, as one understands a language like modern English, would understand it now; would have learned the same language.

There is one exception to this claim of completion. Well, there are many more than one, but let's stay with the single case for the sake of argument. The exception involves music, though, rather than sound – or sound in the form of music. Talking pictures didn't add talk to films, they added the sound of talk, since as many critics have said, silent films were not dumb or mute just because we couldn't hear their conversations. And very few film-makers outside of experimental cinema have taken the opportunity to divorce sound from image when it comes to speech or song. There are the comic and dramatic effects of the plot of *Singin' in the Rain* (1952), which is about the arrival of sound in the American studios, and there are the disturbances of narrative memory in *Last Year at Marienbad* (1961), but generally the sound of talk has been mapped on to the image of talkers – an enhancement of realism but not a change of film language.

There was plenty of music in the silent era, but it was in the movie-house not on the film track. That track itself put thousands of local musicians out of work, and meant that filmgoers all over the world could hear the same high-quality orchestras and compositions. We might now think that such severe standardization was not so wonderful, and want to salute the talent of at least some of those hard-working pianists inventing or plagiarizing variable sounds to go with moving images night after night. But early audiences apparently just loved the chance of getting Toscanini and Max Steiner instead of the local music teacher.

The placement of music in the soundtrack rather than in the cinema or hall does produce new forms of film language. We can think of theme music – the swooping sounds (composed by Max Steiner, Bernard Herrmann, and John Williams) that instantly bring *Gone With the Wind* (1939) or *Vertigo* (1958) or *E.T.* (1982) to mind. But what we might call signalling music is more important as language, a set of idioms that haunted films from the late 1940s to the 1960s, and that have (more or less) vanished because we learned too well how to read them, so that they came to feel like underlining on pages we would rather read clean, or provide with our own emphasis. I have in mind all the carefully stylized sounds meaning that a monster was approaching, that a journey into memory was about to begin, that our heroine was distraught, that the weather was bad, that the cavalry might not make it. Often, such music was associated with particular characters, one for each of them, like a Wagnerian leitmotiv.

The most interesting moments in this language, perhaps, occurred when the film-maker played with our expectations about it. We hear, for example, the sound of Chopin waltzes in an upper-class drawing room in Renoir's *Rules of the Game* (1939). Very fitting, these socialites are having a party. Except that as the camera takes us downstairs, we learn that the music is not Renoir's ornamentation but local programming within the story: it's what the servants are listening to on the radio. Similarly, in Hitchcock's *Rear Window* (1954), the music (by Franz Waxman) we keep hearing is coming not from the outer space of the studio but a neighbouring apartment. In the finest and broadest of such instances, the characters in Mel Brooks's *High Anxiety* (1977) suddenly seem to *hear the soundtrack*, and are appropriately bothered. Then the car they are in is overtaken by a bus containing a symphony orchestra playing John Morris's music at full strength.

These wonderful touches certainly suggest how much can be done with music in films; but they also suggest how much is not being done, so if there is a real addition to film language here, it is after all a relatively modest one.

Real magicalism

It is customary and convenient in the history of film to distinguish between two tendencies, present from the start: realism and magic, represented respectively by the work of the Lumière Brothers and the extraordinary camera games of Georges Meliès. What I have been saying so far suggests not an abandonment of this distinction, which is significant in all kinds of ways, but a rethinking of some of the sites where the two tendencies meet.

Meliès made *Le Voyage dans la lune* (1902) and a number of films full of tricks and fantasies – the most entertaining today are perhaps the ones where a single head is shared by a number of characters (four in one film, a whole orchestra in another) – but he also reconstructed historical occasions, such as key moments in the Dreyfus Affair. The Lumière Brothers filmed a good deal of ordinary life as it was being lived, but one of their most brilliant works is often screened in a version that shows a demolished wall rising again out of its own ruins. It's worth pausing over this film, which is even more revealing of what cinema can do than the old *Tempest* is; and a good deal more direct than *Duck Soup*.

First, we see the preparations for demolition, and then the job itself. A man hacks away at the wall with a pick-axe, a sort of battering ram is screwed up against the other side. The effect is truly documentary, we are looking at a piece of the material world, a built object, or a building's last claim to be a building, as it tilts and topples into dust. We are there. Or they were there. They saw it and filmed it, and it happened in real time. All this is literally true, there is no trickery, the effect of the real is a reflection of the reality of the real. But then the same action is suddenly projected backwards, apparently without a cut. The dust settles and the wall slowly rises into the air, returns to its original condition. If we saw only the end of the film, we would say a wall was being born, not built; conjured up like the walls of a city of myth. The trick of reverse projection is simple, and was discovered very early in the history of the cinema, but the effect is amazing, a feat of genuine animation. What's more, the event really happened, just not in this sequence or direction. What we are seeing is at once quite impossible and perfectly real.

We could revert then to Cavell's argument that something is always there in front of the camera – the argument for the overwhelming sense of such a presence – without having to make any immediate judgement about the actual spatial or material reality involved. The distinction would be between, on one level, the camera playing straight and the camera being up to something; and in an exact parallel, between our being asked to believe we are seeing unfixed reality, and our being invited to wonder how the trick was played. The old distinction, in other words, wouldn't exactly name two tendencies, it would name two poles, with almost no film pitched purely at either end. All film would inhabit a space between realism and magical realism, where realism is not fidelity to the real but an invincible simulation of such fidelity, and magical realism is a means of making the most impossible events look real on their own terms. This way it is easy to think of *Nanook of the North* (1922) and *Avatar* (2009) as belonging to the same medium, and even of both as located somewhere not all that far from the middle of the spectrum.

This argument also works with cartoons; indeed, cartoons help us to see what the argument is actually about. What is real to us in

Young Mr Lincoln, in *The Tempest*, in the proliferating Groucho Marx disguises, in the falling and rising wall, is not the substance of these worlds, the river, the sea, the nightshirt, the bricks – as if the films were just photographs. What is real is the movement, and in cartoons what's plausible is not how the rabbits and cats and mice and coyotes look but how they travel through space. Even the unreal has realistic ways of getting around, and that's what gifted animators devise.

Animation indeed may be the secret of film, if film has a secret. This thought, which would once have been anathema to anyone who cared about cinema, has become almost fashionable. Sean Cubitt, the author of *The Cinema Effect*, developing an argument much fuller and grander than mine, suggests almost casually that we shall one day 'recognize that the photomechanical cinema is a brief interlude in the history of the animated image'. In the first days of cinema, as Donald Crafton reminds us in his wonderful book *Before Mickey*, animation meant not the activation of graphics but trick photography that allowed objects to seem to move of their own accord. It wasn't until around 1914 that animation became associated with comics, and 'drawings that move'. 'No one knows', Crafton writes, 'who first discovered that screen motion could be deliberately synthesized by making single-frame exposures', but the discovery is inseparable from the pleasure of so many early films. A perfect example is provided by whole series of works based on the setting of the haunted hotel. Meliès made five such films between 1896 and 1903, and there was an English *Haunted Castle* of 1897, although the American *Haunted Hotel* (1907), by James Stuart Blackton, was the most successful, and one of the chief reasons why animation was for some time known in France as '*le mouvement américain*'. Each film had some version of the traveller arriving at an inn to find himself entertained only by invisible ghosts, or more precisely, entertained by objects usually thought to be inanimate. Unguided by any hand, even a ghostly one, a knife sliced through a loaf; a wine bottle tilted and poured its contents into a waiting glass.

Chairs and tables and pictures flew about, beds were made and unmade. For some of these effects, borrowed from the stage, one had to use unseen wires. For others, all one had to do was stop the camera, move the objects slightly, and take another shot. It seemed like a miracle at the time; in January 2010, a seven-year-old girl in Glasgow showed me the animation film she had made with her toys and her father's mobile phone. Admittedly, this still seemed like a miracle to me, if not to her.

In 1934, writing of cartoons and not animation in its very early film sense, Panofsky glossed the verb 'animate' as meaning to 'endow lifeless things with life, or living things with a different kind of life', and Crafton correctly insists that such endowing needs an endower. Our sense 'that life is somehow being created' before our eyes 'does not arise from a mystical "something in the form itself" or from a vague "virtue" of the medium'. Nevertheless, Crafton is willing to talk of the attraction of 'movement in itself', and links film animation with the invention of planes and cars, 'objects moving with what seemed to be their own internal life'. What he calls a subspecies of film – already a controversial point, since many scholars and critics do not regard cartoons as films at all – seems to contain within it an explanation of at least one intimate and recurring effect of all the other subspecies.

I'm thinking of those many moments in film when we seem to witness the birth of film itself, when the arrival of the first moving picture seems to be repeated on film. We only seem to see this birth, but the impression can be startling, and can carry us beyond anything required by the immediate narrative occasion. The most famous instance would be the rearing up of the stone lions in Eisenstein's *Battleship Potemkin* (1925), but I shall also name, pretty much at random, the moments when the monster first twitches into life in *Frankenstein* (1931), when the somnambulist Cesare opens his eyes in *The Cabinet of Dr Caligari* (1919), when the otherwise still frames of Chris Marker's *La Jetée* (1962) are interrupted by a single shot taken with a movie camera, when the corpse in the car boot in *Goodfellas* (1990) turns out to be alive, when the supposedly dead monster in countless horror movies comes back for one more attack on our peace of mind. You will think of many more examples.

I said earlier that nothing ever dies on film. The thought is already a little hyperbolic, but I'd like to take it one stage further. Accepting for the moment Roland Barthes' passionate argument that photographs always and only tell us a story of death (they say 'That is dead, and that is going to die'), I'd like to propose something like the reverse for the cinema. What is inanimate comes to life there, what is alive is seen as alive, and what is dead can always come back. This suggestion may seem to contradict Laura Mulvey's definition of cinema as 'death 24 times a second', but I believe it complements it. The recurring death is real, and so is the irresistible appearance of returning movement. There has to be a lot of life in something that can keep dying at that speed.

We could take the end of Brian de Palma's *Carrie* (1976) as an allegorical representation of this claim. The camera shows us the grave of the girl who has caused all the trouble, the story is over. And then out of the ground, in close-up, a living hand rises to clutch the ankle of the person standing there, and to rattle the nerves of every member of the audience who thought it was safe to go home. As this example suggests, animation is not always a positive factor, and in films too we can find the melancholy Barthes explores in photographs. The repeated rebirths of Lauren Bacall or James Stewart, or more precisely, their failure to age within any given film, can remind us how old or how dead they are now. But Barthes' curious point about the cinema can be turned against him. He says cinema is not melancholy, just '"normal", like life', because it takes pictures and moves on. That is, he can find in the cinema 'the melancholy of photography itself' only when he stops the film physically or mentally. But then, by the same token, the film that doesn't stop or won't stop will always picture life for us. It is not an art-form for grieving persons, but only for those who are excited by or afraid of movement. This is another reason to remember that nothing moves in a film frame; only a succession of frames creates movement. Photography stops life, and film, apparently recording life's movement, actually starts it again: a little resurrection every time.

This mythology of rebirth is beautifully orchestrated and thematized at the beginning of Vincente Minnelli's *The Band Wagon* (1953). Fred Astaire, a once famous singer and dancer, arrives in New York on a train. There are crowds of reporters waiting there, so perhaps, he suspects for a moment, he is not the has-been he believes he has become. No such luck. The reporters are there for Ava Gardner. Astaire grins as only he knows how, and starts to walk along the platform towards the exit. His walk is not exactly jaunty or cheery but it is easy and stylish, it is a walk that is already a modest form of dance. His right arm swings comfortably, as if he was conducting an invisible band. And he sings, creating a musical number without dance – or if you prefer, a number with all the dance he needs. The song is 'By Myself', it has a graceful, looping melodic line, and the lyric tells us a wry but not depressing story ('I'll go my way by myself / All alone in a crowd'). It's not exactly a heroic story either; being by oneself is not an ideal condition, only an aspect of the way things are. But it's the filming of the walk that matters, that reveals something only film can show us. Well, perhaps we might catch a glimpse of such a walk in actual life, if we were in the right spot and had an idea of grace. But then we would think life was behaving like a movie. What Minnelli is giving us here is animation in its purest, calmest aspect. Astaire the passenger becomes Astaire the performer – he is a living thing endowed with a different kind of life, in Panofsky's terms – and he does it just by lengthening or loosening his stride. He is his own past and present, the artist whose best days are over, and the artist who will always be himself. We are indeed a long way from the melancholy of photography.

Chapter 2
Trusting the image

Lucky stars

Federico Fellini said that as a child he believed feature films were entirely made up, plot, dialogue, and all, by the actors who worked in them; he didn't know there was such a thing as a director. Of course, he soon recognized his mistake, and made a whole distinguished career out of its obverse; but his childhood vision was not entirely wrong, and is worth lingering over for several reasons.

First, many moviegoers have never thought about the role of the director, even if they have vaguely supposed such a creature must exist. 'Name ten directors' would be quite a hard test even for many people who love films, and have spent much of their lives watching them. I was devoted to westerns as a child, musicals when I was a little older, and I knew all the actors' names, but my curiosity didn't run to the way the films were put together. Now I know that Stanley Donen directed Gene Kelly in *Singin' in the Rain* and *It's Always Fair Weather* (1955), and that Vincente Minnelli directed *An American in Paris* (1951); but I still have to reach for a reference book to tell you who directed the wonderful string of Hopalong Cassidy films, starring William Boyd, that formed my moral imagination when my schoolmates were reading Jane Austen. (For the record, George Archainbaud directed the last dozen or so of the more than 60 Hopalong Cassidy movies, and Howard Bretherton directed the first six.)

I can remember the year, if not the exact day, when I awoke from Fellini's illusion and started paying attention to directors' names. It was hard work, it didn't come naturally. The year was 1959, when I saw Bergman's *The Magician* (1958), and I caught up with the same director's *Wild Strawberries* (1957) and Fellini's *La Strada* (1954). That meant I was ready for Fellini's *La Dolce Vita*, Godard's *Breathless*, Antonioni's *L'Avventura*, and Bergman's *The Virgin Spring*, all 1960. By 1961, when I saw Buñuel's *Viridiana* and Antonioni's *La Notte*, I could pretend I had always known that the director was the central agent of the art of film. But I hadn't, and this earlier non-knowledge is still part of my experience of what I see on a screen, as it is of that of many others. To borrow a distinction I'll return to later, we might say that cinephiles think about directors while moviegoers concentrate on the actors. There is no reason why one person can't occupy both positions, but the positions are not the same.

Second, actors do make films, in the sense that their faces and shapes are the objects that are blown up to giant size on the screen, and they are the ones who are exposed to everything such illumination and fame may create. 'It was Michelle Pfeiffer, after all', John Gregory Dunne says in *Monster*, his book about the making of the film *Up Close and Personal* (1996), 'who was going to be twenty-five feet tall up there on the big screen in a darkened theater, not us'; and Chris Marker is supposed to have claimed that 'It's not a movie unless the people on the screen are larger than those who watch it'. Actors are the language of film, or a large part of that language: most of its nouns, so to speak. Famous directors like to make disparaging remarks about actors. 'Actors are cattle', Hitchcock is said to have said, and then mischievously pretended he had been misquoted. What he had meant, he now claimed, was that actors should be treated like cattle. Luis Buñuel once remarked that the spider in the opening scene of *Susana* (1950) was the best actress he ever had. But even these directors are dependent on actors as language, and the language can often talk back.

We can get a sense of the importance of actors – as language, even prior to any thought of a particular performance – by a simple thought experiment. We imagine, for example, that Steve McQueen had taken the part he was offered in *Apocalypse Now* (1979), and we picture him in Marlon Brando's place as Colonel Kurtz. This is not just alternative casting, it's another film entirely.

A third reason for the centrality of actors is that they are often the ones who get films made, at least the ones that are expensive to make, since it is actors' names that attract investors and bring in the money. Big names come in and out of fashion, and the cash follows their trail. Altman's *The Player*, again, offers a good, satirical portrait of the tone: names are dropped (Bruce Willis, Julia Roberts), no one tries to sell a film story without linking it to a star, and suggesting at the same time that they know how to work a special connection to that person. And this third reason for thinking about actors, of course, takes us back to the first: movies invest in what they imagine audiences want to watch.

The notion of the film star has several layers. Most simply, a star is someone who repeatedly gets leading roles in movies; the glamour of the cinema, whether in Hollywood, Bollywood, or Hong Kong, does the rest. A star is the film equivalent of a divo or diva in opera or politics, and is allowed to misbehave accordingly. We are supposed to wonder, as a recent biography does, whether Warren Beatty can really have slept with 12,775 women – our curiosity is part of who 'Warren Beatty' is. But then, this sense of the star quietly dissolves into another one. A star is a construction, a fabrication of the publicity engines of an industry, and in the good old days the legendary life spun out by gossip columns and studio press releases was as important as the story of any film the star acted in – and indeed, was often the same story as that of the films he or she was most famous for. One of the more familiar star stories is that of the clash between the real life and the studio projection, the tale of Norma Jean Baker lurking in and finally crushed by the legend of Marilyn Monroe. Or the desperate narrative evoked by Rita Hayworth's bleak and witty remark: 'Every man I've known has fallen in love with Gilda' – the title character of her notorious 1946 movie – 'and wakened with me'. But there were stars who seem not to have experienced this division. They were the fiction the studios painted, and no one else.

Stars are myths as well as leading players, and their myths often have more than a touch of sadness or disaster in them. The very title of *A Star is Born* (1954), once we connect it to the plot of the film, which includes James Mason's suicide and the endless suffering behind the bravery of Judy Garland's good cheer, hints at the cost of fame, at an irremediable loss at the heart of so much glitz and luck. It's as if we want stars to pay for the good fortune we have lent them, as if this particular fairy story requires a miserable ending.

But stars – some stars – are not only myths and not only fabrications. 'Stars matter', Richard Dyer writes, 'because they act out aspects of life that matter to us; and performers get to be stars when what they act out matters to enough people.' There are shallow fairy tales and deep fairy tales, and stars play in both. We can't do without them and they can't do without us. And in many cases, it feels as if the stars themselves rather than the studio have created their lasting image, in an act of genuine self-fashioning over time. If we think of the figures Laura Mulvey has in mind when she suggests that 'the years around the centenary [of the birth of cinema] saw the death of the last great Hollywood stars' – she names Marlon Brando, Katharine Hepburn, and Gregory Peck – we have to acknowledge the stars' own contribution to their status. Brando was not a studio creation, although his prolifically squandered and recurringly recovered talent told a desperate story any myth-making studio would have been proud of; Hepburn turned a string of roles, good and bad, into a portrait of the person she had decided to be. Peck – a much lesser star, in my view – projected a dogged, slightly slow-witted decency never more visible than when he was supposed to be a bad guy, as in *The Boys from Brazil* (1978), in which he plays, if that's the right word, Joseph Mengele. Of course, we may want to believe that Hollywood has had more recent stars, and will have more in the future. But these examples certainly help us to see what a complex creation a star can be, and how many factors go into his or her making: talent, looks, luck, scripting, roles, money, and our ongoing need for help in the vicarious living of our own lives.

We get a slightly different sense of the star if we go further back in history, and think of figures like Greta Garbo and Marlene Dietrich. Here a certain distance – created by hazy photography and certain aloofness in Garbo's case, by carefully crafted roles and an often withering irony in the case of Dietrich – reminds us of the origin of the metaphor, the far glitter of what isn't our world. These creatures don't tell our stories, even when we are at our most ambitious or fanciful. Before we got the stars we deserved, we had the stars we couldn't reach. The very notion of the star, indeed, bears a relation to the elaborate and exotic architecture of movie-houses, which I'll return to. It's as if the fantastic nature of film provoked fantasies all around it, about the personnel in the pictures and in the gaudy places where they were shown. 'You are not dreaming' is a subtitle in a French Surrealist film, *The Star of the Sea* (1928). The slogan of Hollywood might be 'You are not dreaming but we certainly hope you feel you are'. It is for this reason that the French philosopher Alain Badiou can say the cinema is 'an instrument for transforming the actor into a star', or that this is at least 'a possible definition of the cinema'.

There are plenty of untransformed actors in the movies, though, and the distinction between actor and star is implicit in everything I have been saying in the last few pages. The star can do things with a role but cannot disappear into it; there are no invisible stars in the film firmament. This is not a weakness, but it is a fact. And a movie star is not really a personage, like a great actor on the live stage. With stage actors, we remember their performances, not their parts. Movie stars are not really performing, but they are projecting; the parts they play and the gossip they generate become a combined, continuing story about their lives, which in turn defines who they are as stars.

And film actors? Of course, not all film actors are stars in the senses I have just elaborated – and plenty of stars are not actors in any sense at all – but they are, in a curious way, both more and less themselves than any stage actor can afford to be. More themselves because whatever their disguises and accents, the camera will almost always identify them personally, tie them unmistakably to their body and time and place. Just think of how American most of the characters look in a Hollywood epic set in ancient Rome or Egypt, say, and how irrevocably they belong to the 1950s. And these actors are less themselves because all we see of them are vast projections, ghosts of another time and place, not Rome or Egypt, but a brightly lit studio on a mid-20th-century day that will never return. They can't hide their wrinkles from us, or their excesses of make-up; and they can't get any older, or fix their speech or clothes.

Film acting, as is often said, is an art of understatement. Stage actors usually overdo things on screen, like an opera singer putting too much vibrato into Cole Porter. The camera will take over almost all the work if it is allowed to, and stillness on the screen often speaks more eloquently than gesture. But there is stillness and stillness, and the art of understatement is still an art. Characters in the films of Yasujiro Ozu, for example, frequently sit and do nothing but think; just as the river in *Young Mr Lincoln* does nothing but flow. But not every sitting person in the world or in movies appears to be thinking, and not every river helps us to think about grief. Generally, film actors who try to look as if they are caught up in thought give the impression of people about to have a fit. Roland Barthes makes fun of the fact that most of the actors in Joseph Mankiewicz's *Julius Caesar* (1953) are sweating. This, he says, is because they are supposed to be thinking. 'To sweat is to think – which evidently rests on the postulate...that thought is a violent, cataclysmic operation, of which sweat is only the most benign symptom.'

But the combination of camera, director, the right story, and the right actor can do everything that needs to be done without seeming to do much at all. We don't even need the Japanese delicacy of Ozu, whose characters suffer so much with so much punctilious decorum. John Ford does with the same with John Wayne in *The Searchers* (1956), as the actor/character tries to find a facial expression to match his bafflement at feeling what he is not supposed to feel. And in *Death in Venice* (1971), which contains what is, I suppose, *the* virtuoso performance of thought on screen in Western cinema, Dirk Bogarde, or to be precise, the combined labours of Dirk Bogarde, Luchino Visconti, Gustav Mahler, and the cameraman Pasquale de Santis, trace an extremely complex flow of amazement, relief, and guilty pleasure with scarcely a movement of an eyebrow. Literally, we see a face and a body and a sweep of water, with plenty of moody music in the soundtrack. Effectively, we are looking into the mind of a man who has found an excellent excuse (his luggage has been sent to the wrong place) for doing what he knows he shouldn't do: stay on in Venice and stalk the boy he admires.

It's all true

There are films without actors – that is, without professional actors, and also without persons playing any kind of fictional part. There are films – many of them made for television in recent years – where the only characters are birds or elephants or jaguars or patches of landscape. I put the matter this way because I don't believe there are films without characters. In political or historical documentaries, the characters are versions of the figures we know from other documents, and in nature films the characters are whatever creatures or pieces of the earth we are invited to watch in action – or inaction. In Luis Buñuel's documentary film *Land without Bread* (1932), the location (named in the Spanish title as *Las Hurdes*) is the hero and the villain, it survives and destroys its human inhabitants, and it marks them far more severely and completely than they could ever hope to mark or change it.

Las Hurdes Altas, the High Hurdes, is a cluster of villages in west central Spain not far from Salamanca. In the 1930s, some 6,000 people (or 10,000 according to the commentary on some prints of the work) lived in 52 hamlets. There was no folklore in these communities, Buñuel says, no pictures or songs: only disease, hunger, and isolation. We are about to enter what Fredric Jameson very aptly calls 'an atrocious and inverted Shangri-la'.

However, Las Hurdes preserve just enough culture to make it a mockery: a little geometry, the concept of property. 'These children are famished', the voice-over commentary murmurs, 'but they are taught that the sum of the angles of a triangle equals two right angles'. There is a cut to a close-up of a row of small bare feet dangling down from a rough bench. A child writes carefully on the blackboard *Respetad los bienes ajenos*, 'Respect the goods of others', which the commentary sardonically calls 'the golden rule'.

We arrive through a range of rocky, dusty-looking mountains, and our first glimpse of the settlement is a shot of the roofs of a village, squat and blind, a heap of stone dwellings like a jumbled cemetery or, as the commentary says, like an assembly of 'fabulous turtles'. We learn later that many of the houses have no chimneys or windows, so that smoke from domestic fires filters out through walls and doors.

The film details aspects of life in these communities: education, as we have seen, agriculture, disease, death. An ancient toothless crone is seen giving suck to a baby. We have just time to absorb the grotesqueness of the picture before the narrator's voice informs us that the woman is 32 years old. We then come across a little girl lying in an empty, unpaved street, and are told she has been lying there for three days. A hand enters the frame, opens the girl's mouth to reveal gums and tonsils wildly inflamed. 'Unfortunately', the narrator says, 'we could do nothing for her. Two days later we returned to the village and were told the little girl was dead.'

Why could they do nothing for her? Couldn't they have taken her to the world of doctors and hospitals from which they had come? I raise the question because it seems to me the question Buñuel is waiting for us to ask, and because it has something to do with a lurking immunity or helplessness of film – of the medium, that is, not just this work. Jameson says, 'the documentary film has a kind of nostalgia for engagement, for political commitment, built into itself as a kind of inner distance or absence, as a kind of guilty conscience'. I would add only that the commitment doesn't have to be political and that it is thanks to film, of course, that I can worry about a long dead child, and about what a now dead director showed me of her last days. Still, I do worry, as I couldn't if the film was fiction, or if I was convinced this scene was staged. The documentary film can offer only a pledge of its representation of reality, as Aufderheide says. But the pledge can be more than enough.

I should say something, though, about a famous staged scene in the film. The Hurdanos get their milk from mountain goats. The goats jump about on the local cliffs, and like everything else in this world, they are at risk, always close to death, and sometimes more than close. At one point, we see a goat in medium shot, about to jump from one rocky place to another. Then we see the goat falling in long shot, down the face of a tall cliff: it has missed its footing. Immediately, we see another shot of the goat falling (*a* goat falling, the identity of the goat is exactly what's implied but only implied) but taken from the place of the goat's failed jump: the goat is falling directly below us and away from us. There is no way a camera could have transported itself so immediately to this spot – or indeed been waiting, since that's where the goat was, and we are suddenly in a fiction film, some early Spanish version of Italian neo-realism, or a relative of certain famous action photographs now thought to have been carefully set up by the photographer. Presumably, one goat is photographed as it jumps; another (I hope already dead) goat is thrown from the cliff in front of the camera, which was waiting for this act, not pursuing it. Buñuel himself, asked about this scene, was surprised that anyone might think it represented unarranged reality – how could it? But he didn't regard it as less real for being arranged: goats were dying in Las Hurdes, whatever he and his camera were doing.

The Hurdanos, short of potatoes, often eat cherries before they are ripe: a source of dysentery. They create strips of plantable land by the river, but have to transport decent soil from the mountain in order to do this. We watch them hauling sacks of earth down a bare crag, forming narrow fields, the whole scene an image of pitiless geography, to adapt Buñuel's phrase about the faces in Dreyer's *Passion of Joan of Arc*. Soon after this portrait of the Hurdanos' fidelity to what he later called 'this hell which belongs to them', Buñuel presents us with the most brilliant sequence of shots in the film, and one of the great triumphs of montage in general: Eisenstein meets Surrealism, so to speak. We see the dry bed of a stream, a patch of muddy water, revealed in a scooped sample to be dense with insects. Suddenly, there is a cut to the pages of a medical textbook, with illustrations and descriptions of different types of mosquito. The anopheles, we are told in an impartial scholarly voice-over, carries malaria, which is rife in the Hurdes Altas. Then, without warning, the film cuts to a medium shot of a trembling man, all shakes, malaria in action. It is like being tipped out of medical school into the middle of the plague, and it is an effect, I believe, that only film can allow, and that only a great director would have thought of. No photograph, for example, could have shown the actual shakes of the quivering man, and only a film could shift in this way from still page to live person, from pictured insect to triumphant disease. For a moment, it seems to me, the medium sheds its helplessness. It is science that stands aloof, film that gives us the immediate, trembling creature.

As the film ends, there is a last shot of the dusty mountains at dawn, and the commentary wryly says, 'After a stay of two months in Las Hurdes, we left the region'. William Rothman reads this shot as suggesting that 'the land of the Hurdanos has no boundaries. The camera reveals no way out, no world "outside" this impoverished region.' This is a powerful interpretation, and matches Rothman's sense that the horror of the Hurdanos' existence is 'our horror, too'. And it is true that the film places us metaphorically in a world without exit. But literally we have never lived there or, most of us, been anywhere like it, so the film catches us between an imaginative identification of the kind Rothman evokes and the radical privilege that watching such a film offers to us. Documentary works regularly and usefully entangle us in these ambiguities of ethnography. If the 'others' were not to some degree like us, we couldn't care about them. If we really were the others, the very notion of caring wouldn't come up.

Jean Rouch, director of the classic *Chronicle of a Summer* (1961) and many other films, says that for him

> there is almost no boundary between documentary films and films of fiction. The cinema, the art of the double, is already the transition from the real world to the imaginary world, and ethnography, the science of the thought systems of others, is a permanent crossing point from one conceptual universe to another.

'Almost no boundary' is not the same as no boundary, and of course, given what I have tried to say about the narrowness of the gap between the magical representation of the real and the real representation of magic, I have to echo Rouch's thought in large measure. In films, there are only replicas of things, even if some of those replicas are imprints rather than copies of the real, and when I speak of characters in films, I mean everything in whose life we are invited to take an interest. We can't take an interest without using our imagination, and this is as true of the real as it is of anything else. What's more, all films, documentary or not, are shaped by someone's imagination before we see them, angled, edited, pitched, paced. The subjective and the objective vision are not at odds here, not even opposites. The subjective vision, attentive to what is not itself, creates for us whatever objectivity is available to mere mortals. Or at least it may create it, and if it won't, nothing else will. As Jacques Rancière suggests, one question to ask about any documentary is what sort of fiction it is. Fiction here would not mean myth or falsehood but imaginative arrangement, and the interest would be in referencing reality rather than, as in self-declared fictional works, evoking an illusion of reality. Even Holocaust deniers, Rancière adds, don't need to deny a lot of facts. What they need to deny is the link that turns those facts into history.

Still, there is a boundary between documentaries and fiction films, just as there is a difference between Buñuel's unfalsifiable shot of the shaking man and the fancy construction of the goat's fall. It would be easy to say what this difference is if we could believe in the old myth of photography's inevitable fidelity to the real, and conscript it once again for the cause of film. The man really is shaking, and the camera is there, unable not to record the shakes. But frankly, the man could have been a brilliant actor, and the point is that *we just don't think he might have been* – not that we couldn't think it, or that it couldn't be the case. It is a question, I suggest, not of the authenticity of the camera but of our trust in the image. And what we trust is the claim of the documentary at its strongest and firmest: that its pictures and stories stem from a world that is not only like ours but is ours, historically verifiable, visitable, a world that has left marks for us to find if we care to look. There is a difference between fiction and fact, even if they are always infiltrating each other, and even if pure cases of either are hard to come by. The shivering man is the illusion we cannot take for an illusion.

If this man seems to defy or sideline our disbelief, the images of Alain Resnais' *Night and Fog* (1955) provide something like the reverse challenge: they defy our belief, although everything about them says they are true. Philip Lopate, among others, has wondered whether this film is perhaps not a documentary but rather an essay, that is, not so much descriptive as speculative. I've been suggesting, in effect, that all documentary films are essays, even (especially) when they imagine they are not, when they picture themselves as just telling it (whatever it may be) like it is. *Night and Fog*, however, is an unusually thoughtful and delicate essay.

The film very quickly sets up a contrast between its use of colour and its use of black and white images. Colour signifies the present tense, the time of the making of the film, the time of its narration, 1955, ten years after the war and the discovery of the full secret of the German concentration camps. There is something cautiously, deliberately bland about the colour frames, even when the camera drops quietly from its view of a blue sky to include a barbed wire fence, and then the empty fields and disused buildings of a former camp. This is now, and then was then. Can we get there from here? The answer is complicated. We can get there easily, we have the pictures, and the film shows them to us in plenty: film clips, photographs, raw footage, arranged in mounting degrees of horror as the film progresses. And we can scarcely get there at all, it's too far away in moral space and imaginative time. Every aspect of the film is carefully subordinated to this double response.

The trains filled with prisoners shown to us at the beginning seem haunted and threatening, of course, but also banal, too ordinary to move us beyond an old sorrow. The sight of German soldiers standing around, chatting, smoking, as the trains are loaded, is in its way more shocking. We've seen these trains before, the trains have stories, but how could these men, at the time, think what was happening was ordinary, all in a day's (not very hard) work? This question is not answered but rather amplified by a series of images borrowed from Leni Riefenstahl's *Triumph of the Will* (1935), showing Hitler taking a salute at a march-past, and what seems to be a unanimous supportive nation filling the screen. The strutting soldiers look as if they are caught up in a vast, harsh ballet, which in turn suggests unison, order, the unquestioned road.

The commentary, written by Jean Cayrol and spoken by Michel Bouquet, takes an ironic line about all this ordinariness, as if to get excited or emotional were dangerous – as if the film and the voice might lose control then, or as if the banality of evil had to be allowed its full range of banality. It is in this spirit that the commentary speaks of the construction of the camps as commercial building projects ('A concentration camp is built like a grand hotel. You need contractors, estimates, competitive offers. And no doubt friends in high places'), and takes the architectural styles of watchtowers as the occasion for a bleak joke: 'The Swiss style. The garage style. The Japanese model. No style at all.' A documentary image accompanies each of these mock identifications, as if the sequence were part of an academic lecture. The joke, in this context, expresses more outrage than mere outrage could.

The central moment of the film's present tense, the expression of the limits of what film can do when the past is past, takes the form of a very long tracking shot along a row of empty bunks in a former camp. The challenge is to imagine these bunks full of living people – who are going to die, and who are now dead, in Roland Barthes' formulation. Except that, since this a movie, they can't die because they can't get into the picture, the moving camera has no room or time for them. And yet, of course, they can't live either, for exactly the same reason. They are not there. The camera's exclusion of them becomes our difficulty in remembering them. The commentary is particularly eloquent at this point.

These wooden blocks, these beds where three people slept, these burrows where people hid, where they furtively ate, and sleep itself was a danger – no description, no shot, can restore their true dimension, endless, uninterrupted fear...Only the husk and shade remains of this brick dormitory.

The camera reaches the end of the row, pauses at a blank wall, and starts its journey back along the bunks, 'as if', in William Rothman's words, 'it were its immutable fate to keep endlessly traversing this long row of empty beds'.

The end of the film strikes this note too. We see some old (and now all too sadly familiar) footage of the liberation of the camps. The haunted faces of the living prisoners stare through the barbed wire at what is supposed to be the image of their freedom, the world this side of the fence. The commentary asks, 'Have they been freed? Is daily life going to recognize them (*La vie quotidienne va-t-elle les reconnaître*)?' Not, we notice, are they going to recognize it. There follows some footage of a kapo and two officers denying responsibility, and the commentary asks who then is responsible? We see a pale inmate looking sadly down – at what? – and then we return to a reminder of the horrors we were inspecting just before we saw the liberation footage: skeletal corpses tossed into graves, skulls carried by hand and laid out in rows on the ground, charred bodies, frames full of eyeglasses, shoes, bowls, shaving brushes, female hair, masses of bodies scooped up by a tractor and dumped into a pit – all images in black and white, film and still photographs taken by unimaginable cameramen of the past. Now, after our view of the prisoners awaiting their release, we see three still photographs, or perhaps three different close-ups on a single photograph, showing, once again, corpses piled up and spread out like a medieval engraving, a sort of chaotic dance of death. Then the screen turns to colour, pale green with dots of mauve, a sort of messy Monet, it seems, and the association is not too far from the mark. This is a pond which now covers the burying grounds of one of the camps, a blurred and (in 1955) more or less meaningless image. But then its historical existence vanishes immediately into what the commentary names as its metaphor: 'the cold and opaque water of our bad memory'. 'Who among us', the commentary asks, 'watches from this strange observatory?' – as if the watchtower of a camp had itself become a perspective on the past. There are those who don't believe in any of this, the voice-over continues, and those who believe in it from time to time. And there is whoever 'we' are, the community composed of the makers and viewers of the film, who are described as 'sincerely looking at these ruins', and pretending to believe that such atrocities belong to only one time and one country.

This is part of what we pretend to believe. We are also pretending perhaps that we understand these matters better than we do. But mainly we are struggling, I think, and the film is inviting us to struggle, with whatever separation is represented by the division between the bland, coloured present and the astonishing specificity of the black and white past. We can't deny either element, and we can't combine them. The closing suggestion of the film is that the camps could come into being again at any place or time, and certainly this hint is well meant and well placed. But it's not really what the world felt like in 1955, and in its benevolent and thoughtful way the suggestion is an evasion of the film's own subject. Before we can worry about whether these things can happen again, we have to be convinced they happened once. We are convinced, of course, but in a way that leaves us baffled. Now we do say we can't believe our own eyes; and we mean, as we always do, that we have to believe them but can't deal with what they are seeing. Our situation is neither that of our encounter with the shivering man in *Land without Bread*, nor that created by our viewing the Lumière wall that rises magically from its own dust. In the first case, we are convinced that the man and his illness are as real as anything on a screen can be. In the second, the action is, as I have said, both real and impossible. The horrible images of *Night and Fog* are real and inconceivable. We have trouble in believing in our own belief in them. Our incredulity is both a virtue, a form of fidelity to shock, and a liability, part of what may help these images to fade, as the film's own language suggests, from the violent clarity of the past into the empty haze of the present.

Nations and moments

In 1914, 90% of the films distributed internationally in the world were French; by 1928, 85% were American. This shift is what Jean-Luc Godard is referring to when he says, in his eight-episode video series *Histoire(s) du cinema* (1997–8), that the First World War allowed the American cinema to ruin the French cinema – grimly adding that the Second World War, along with the birth of television, allowed the American cinema 'to finance, that is to say to ruin, all the (national) cinemas of Europe'. This is a piece of the story. Another piece is that a whole cloud of American films, banned from Occupied France, flew in like a revelation after the war, and allowed French cinema to remake itself, and Godard's own movies were a large part of that remaking. No Nicholas Ray and Sam Fuller, we might say, no *Breathless* (1960). The French had Jean Renoir to turn to, but much of André Bazin's film theory, for example, was based on the work of Orson Welles and William Wyler.

It's still true that American films make up a huge chunk of the world market. Early in 2010, *Avatar* was pulled from 1,628 screens in China because it was felt to be getting too much attention – its replacement was a homegrown biopic about Confucius. But if 'US films continue to dominate admissions', as a 2010 UNESCO report states, referring to figures for 2006, there are interesting exceptions, cases where the local product has the edge: India and France. And India is where most films (this figure is for feature-length items) are made: 1,091 in 2006. Nigeria came second with 872 films; the US third with 485. In comparison, 203 films were made in France that year; 104 in the UK. The Nigerian instance is particularly significant, especially for arguments about the possible death and continuing life of the movies because, in the words of the same report, there are 'virtually no formal cinemas' in the country – all viewing is done in some sort of home or improvised setting.

'Trade follows films' is the slogan Godard cites in *Histoire(s)* – but films and nations are not purely economic entities. Siegfried Kracauer, in *From Caligari to Hitler* (1947), argued that a whole German mentality could be divined from the films of a certain period. This sort of critical move can be made too easily, especially with hindsight; but it seems certain that times and places can conjoin to produce quite specific, unrepeatable sets of films: Russian experiment, English comedy, Italian neo-realism, the French New Wave, Brazilian Cinema Novo. Keeping in mind that everything could have been different, and remembering Max Weber's dictum that a belief in national character is a superstition, there is no reason why we can't try to see what some of these conjunctions may mean.

As Kracauer suggests, a string of remarkable German films, from *The Cabinet of Dr Caligari* (1920) through *Nosferatu* (1920) and *Metropolis* (1927) to *The Testament of Dr Mabuse* (1933), had plenty to say to us, through fantasy, about the historical world – about that world as it might be and had in part become. The interpretative claim would be similar to the one Adorno makes about paranoia. 'Something in reality strikes a chord in paranoid fantasy and is warped by it.' The reality of Weimar Germany gives rise to these tilted perspectives, these strange doctors and vampires, who eerily find their imitators in fact.

The situation with neo-realism in Italy was quite different. Too many fears had been fulfilled, and too many extravagant and murderous fantasies had taken over what used to be politics. The series of sombre, truth-telling films that runs from Rossellini's *Rome Open City* (1945) through de Sica's *Bicycle Thieves* (1948) to Visconti's *Rocco and His Brothers* (1960) offered a correction to a thoroughly distorted world – or returned to us a world whose undistorted ordinariness had long been lost from sight. It was not simply a matter of using amateur actors or real locations. The 'real' in these films, as in documentaries, was scrupulously put together, not just picked up by accident or pure technology. The point is that it needed putting together. Indeed, if we don't understand the degree to which reality was felt to have been lost, we can hardly understand the force of these films, and the degree to which such a loss was a matter of dishonour – Godard's suggestion was that 'with *Rome Open City* Italy has simply recovered the right for a nation to look itself in the face'.

The French New Wave was different again. A group of film-makers and would-be film-makers took on the French cinematic establishment, the very notion of the glossy, well-made, expensive film. The flurry of films that appeared – *The Four Hundred Blows* (1959), *The Cousins* (1959), *Breathless* (1960), *Jules and Jim* (1962) – offered a stark, subversive contrast to the smoothly paced work of established directors like René Clément and Claude Autant-Lara, and in part the goal, as in Italy, was a certain realism, a sense of a daily world that had gone missing. But that daily world was quirkier in the French case, truer to youth and rebellion and Hitchcock than to any historical or political agenda. This is the case even when the films have plenty of politics. In Godard's *Le Petit Soldat* (1960), a film set during the Algerian War and much concerned with assassination, torture, and interrogation, Anna Karina says being photographed is like being questioned by the police. This doesn't give any sort of pause to Michel Subor, her friend, who is photographing her. 'Photography is truth', he says authoritatively. The rest of the scene is all about pictures, moving and still. We watch Subor taking his photos, we see all the motions his own still camera can't catch, and of course, we see the moves he himself makes in the process of taking his pictures. We hear Subor in voice-over speaking from a later time; and there are images which cannot be the point of view of any camera in the room, but only of the finished, developed film: they look like completed fashion stills, disturbed only by the faint continuing movement within the frame. Photography and film are the truth, in this context, not because they are honest and simple, but because they offer us multiple perspectives on a reality caught off-guard, and therefore hard to deny as reality. In *Histoire(s) du cinema*, the critic Serge Daney says to Godard that he was lucky to have been born early enough to inherit a film history that was already rich and complicated – and not too late, the implication is, to do something with it.

Japan has had a flourishing film industry since the silent days, and it's hard to pick characteristic examples when so many moments are exemplary. There is a spell though in the 1950s when certain currents of concern gather in the work of very different movie-makers. This is perhaps the place to take up the wager offered by the French director Jacques Rivette.

Rivette thought we should not put Kenji Mizoguchi and Akira Kurosawa together at all because 'you can compare only what is comparable and that which aims high enough'. This is a common line of thought, especially among French critics. Mizoguchi is 'completely Japanese', Rivette says, and Kurosawa is some kind of international adventurer, infected by the viewing of John Ford. We might think that both just chose their ways of being Japanese, since that is what they were, and in the films I want briefly to look at, the very real differences of style between the two men converge on distinctly national preoccupations.

Both *Ugetsu Monogatari* (1953) and *The Hidden Fortress* (1958) are set in times of civil war, and indeed in the same time: the 16th century. Both have a more recent international war in mind, and both picture war as a condition in which deluded men seek profit. The phrases 'money is everything' and 'war is good for business' come from *Ugetsu*, but they could just as easily have come from *The Hidden Fortress*, if anyone in that movie had anything as respectable or as vulgar as a business. There the relevant claim is

4. Not for profit

that one can 'make a fortune from the war'. In both films, two
peasants have hopes and ambitions above their station, which are
roundly mocked and criticized, particularly in the knockabout
performances of certain actors – Sakae Ozawa in *Ugetsu* and
Kamatari Fujiwara in *The Hidden Fortress* – but not finally
dismissed or minimized in the name of an older, less scrambling
social order. That is, neither film endorses the actions of these
troublesome strivers, but both acknowledge them as markers of
significant historical forces and appetites – and no doubt more so
in the 20th century than the 16th.

I mustn't go any further, though, without signalling some of the
huge differences between the works. *Ugetsu* is a quiet, slow, lyrical
film full of death, and *The Hidden Fortress* is an adventure movie
with two clowns at its centre. The peasants' ambitions in
Ugetsu – one man wants to be a samurai, the other to sell pots and

make a packet – turn out to be lethal or desperately damaging, while the two scavengers in *The Hidden Fortress* escape with their lives and at least a small piece of what they wanted: a fraction of the fortune they went to the war to seek. Yet it is in *The Hidden Fortress* that we get a practice run – in a wide-screen format Kurosawa was using for the first time – for the horrific grand-scale massacres of the same director's *Ran* (1985). And in this film as in the later one, characters murmur with what feels like apocalyptic accuracy, 'This is hell', and 'This is the end'.

The two clowns in *The Hidden Fortress* – said to be the models for R2D2 and C3PO in *Star Wars* – are often funny but rarely pleasant. They get caught up in the escape of a princess and a general who is protecting her, there is not a moment when they wouldn't betray these aristocrats if they could, and they repeatedly scheme to rape the princess – not a tendency Princess Leia has to worry about in her escorts. *The Hidden Fortress* is a film, in other words, where classes are required to form a bond and worry about each other; where chivalry saves the day but only because it has become modernized and humanized. Kurosawa said that with his work he wanted to make a film 'full of thrills and fun' – unlike his *Throne of Blood* and *The Lower Depths* (both 1957), in which much darkness was borrowed, respectively, from Shakespeare and Gorky. And he did. But by framing rather than banishing a whole set of contemporary Japanese worries.

The mood of the final scenes of *Ugetsu* is very complex indeed. Genjuro, the potter, has met up, not with a princess but certainly a high-born lady, who falls in love with him, and takes him to live with her. He forgets all about his wife, about everything except his grand romance and the world of grace and delicacy he has magically entered. He then discovers his mistress is a ghost and is horrified, although we are more likely to be drawn to her when we learn that she died too young to know love, and has returned to the world in search of that supposedly universal experience. Finally, after several years, Genjuro leaves the ghost to grief and oblivion, and goes home. The war has destroyed much in the village and his own house is cold and deserted at first sight. Then he finds his wife there after all. She prepares a meal, watches over him as he falls asleep. There is a curious melancholy about her gestures, all photographed as if they were an intricate leavetaking rather than a greeting. We may be baffled by the tone here, however beautiful this sequence looks. But not for long. Morning comes, Genjuro awakes. The house is as cold and deserted as when he saw it on arrival. His wife has been dead for some years, it was her ghost that welcomed him back.

If in *The Hidden Fortress* war is the state of exception that threatens to become the norm, in *Ugetsu* war is the condition that, beyond all vulgar opportunism, permits men to attempt the crossing to the world of dreams. To attempt and achieve it, in one case. But then the world of dreams is also a world of death – doubly so, since it is while you are there that death takes over the world of reality. War is an occasion perhaps not so much for violence as for porousness, an uncertainty of relation between worlds. Mizoguchi never moralizes, but it's hard not to feel he is pointing to moral vulnerabilities, to some deep flaw in current wishing, that makes mistakes as catastrophic as they are, and again, it's hard to think he has only the 16th century in mind.

In Bengali cinema, and especially in the work of Satyajit Ray, we are stylistically and morally quite close to Italian neo-realism: invited into modest, quiet, neglected regions like that of the Apu trilogy – *Pather Panchali* (1955), *Apajarito* (1956), *The World of Apu* (1959). But the rhythms of time and history are different, and we find in Ray an understanding of empire which is a long way from any imperial understanding. This is especially true of the relatively neglected *Chess Players* (1977), Ray's only film in Urdu, and one of very few set in the past.

The movie is everywhere haunted by its slow credit sequence. We see a chess game in close-up from the side, the pieces on the

5. Who is the ghost?

board, and behind them the fallen shapes of pieces taken and removed. Pudgy, beringed hands enter the frame to move a piece, leave the frame again. A witty, rather aloof narrator in voice-over makes the analogy between chess and war, and we are certainly interested in that, and the rest of what the narrator has to say about Lord Dalhousie swallowing pieces of continent on behalf of the East India Company. But there is something about the steady, side-long view of the game itself, the ornate, elegant pieces of red and white ivory, that resists not only allegory but any sort of interpretation, and the movie invites us to think of everything we know that is idle, obsessive, undirected, everything that sits on the margins of history, and fails to grasp the brutal purpose of the rulers of worlds, large and small.

We meet the same material in the film's great set-piece, where Richard Attenborough, as the Company's Agent in Oudh, asks the King of Awadh to sign the treaty which requires his abdication.

We know what each of these men thinks since we have seen them in separate scenes acknowledging in their different ways their own faults and the large wrongness of what is happening. In the long construction of the film's beautiful plot, everything is explained, we know why the scene is so awkward, we know what both men are not saying. We don't forget any of this as we watch the scene. On the contrary, our knowledge of the background informs every moment of the scene. Even so, we see something else, something that is not even a story.

We see the Agent's red-faced embarrassment, his blotchy skin itself a map of empire, we hear the tone of bullying even as we know the man thinks this bullying is wrong. And on the king's face, we see not the responsibility for the disaster he has already fully registered but a sort of melancholy beyond tragedy. Ray's camera returns to these faces, and especially to the king's, with a kind of wondering, baffled curiosity, lingering because it knows there is nothing to do but linger. The timing is essential, the return to the faces, the waiting as the faces do nothing except, so to speak, repeat themselves. Beyond the bullying and the melancholy, the lingering suggests not helplessness but a sort of awe at the intricacies of human complicity, at the way in which everyone gets a role, accepts a role, in the drama no one wants.

The director himself is not complicit in this sad story, but he and we are accomplices in something else: in the bafflement that besets us when we run out of narrative, or of explanations of history. We don't lose them for long, we can't bear to do without them; and they come back in force. That's why movies, lives, and history have narratives, and that's how they sign up for sequential, progressive time. But there is another time, something like the exact opposite of the Messianic moment that Walter Benjamin evokes, that of the sudden, always unexpected apocalypse. Ray's time is the time in which the Messiah cannot come. No one will come, nothing will happen, no meaning will surface. At least, none we don't already

6. Is there a next move?

know. This time is not confined to Ray's movies, of course; but it's hard to think of anyone who understands it better.

Art and experiment

All film was necessarily experimental at first, and the Lumière Brothers thought for some time that one of the main uses of moving pictures might literally be in scientific experiments. And of course, commercial films can be and often are experimental in terms of their technology – think of the wholesale arrival of computer-generated imagery with *Tron* in 1982 (there had been more limited uses earlier), or the many developments in camera and colour possibilities. I would say too that mass entertainment, especially in comedy and suspense, often has an experimental edge – always another trick to try out, you never know what will catch a large audience's imagination. We have seen some of the experiments that dominated the early days of animation.

But by the time the film industry had settled down, it had settled for narrative, and took its task to be primarily one of story-telling – through pictures and title-cards, and then through pictures and sound. In this mode, the possibilities of the new medium as an art-form in itself, a game with or an inquiry into vision, as Dada and Surrealism played with and remade language and longing, got rather short shrift with the general public. If it is important to remember that 'film' for many people means the narrative feature film, it is important too to remember how much else is going on. And has been going on, from Duchamp's *Anemic Cinema* (1925) to the films of Len Lye, Stan Brakhage, and William Kentridge. We are not talking about what came to be known as art films – narrative films of the highbrow persuasion – but about films as forms of visual art – films in which, as Laura Mulvey very well puts it, the maker has 'consistently brought the mechanism and the material of film into visibility, closing the gap between the filmstrip and the screen'.

The last time I saw René Clair's *Entr'acte* (1924) in a public space was in a museum in Barcelona. It ran on a loop in what was largely an exhibition of sculptures, notably those of Juan Muñoz; in another room was Robert Morris's film *Waterman Switch* (dance composition 1965, filmed much later). The connections to be made among the forms of art on offer were quite wonderful. The Clair film looked like an elaborate sculpture that technology was teasing with tricks of movement; the Muñoz sculptures, especially *The Prompter* or *The Wasteland*, looked like movies that had wound down and found themselves frozen into decaying tableaux. 'You have to come, to look, to despair and smile', Muñoz wrote about his work.

Entr'acte, which begins as a zany film narrative that inspired Luis Buñuel and many other avant-gardistes, ends up in virtual abstraction, and so looks like a rapid, unintentional history of experimental film, or a piece of that history. At the start, there are various antics with an unmoored cannon moving about on its own, and two men jumping about in such slow motion that they seem to be flying. After various other gags, another man is killed and the film settles down to record his funeral procession. Well, to attend to the mutation of this procession. An old-fashioned hearse waits outside a church, but as we look for the presumed horse, the camera shifts sideways to show a camel between the shafts. It's a good surrealist joke, but not out of line as surrealist jokes go. Not as outrageous as the Buñuelesque move – this is before Buñuel had had the chance to make any moves at all on film – which shows a legless man in a small box on wheels, paddling himself along with this hands, anxious to be part of what has become a chase. After several shots, during which we wonder whether we should be finding this funny at all, the man loses his patience, gets up out of the box, full-limbed, and starts running.

Meanwhile, back at the funeral, various solemn-looking people wearing formal attire and many of them having floral wreaths about their necks, descend a set of steps and line up behind the hearse. These people are played by a whole crew of the director's friends, including Marcel Duchamp, Man Ray, and Francis Picabia, the last of whom wrote the script. Now an extraordinary thing happens, easily described as an event but with an effect almost impossible to evoke. The camel pulls away at a steady pace, and the people in the procession start to...leap along after the bier in exaggerated slow motion. Except that it doesn't look like running in slow motion, it looks like a new way of paying one's respects, a local custom. These folks are just seriously sailing through the air after the corpse, and one old lady in particular is throwing herself energetically into the task, legs very straight, a sort of floating dead march. This sequence goes on, shot from different angles, and selecting different members of the group, for a minute and a half. One can have all kinds of responses to this gag, but it seems funny beyond anything the basic trick might suggest, and my double response has always been: only cinema could do this, and this is what cinema should be doing, at least some of the time.

At one point, the hearse rolls free and takes off sans camel down the road. The hearse rides a roller-coaster, whizzes through a forest, and it is at this stage that the film becomes almost entirely abstract: shapes and lines whirr and flicker by, we see the world from the hearse's point of view, and although we can parse those shapes into leaves, rails, and parapets if we like, that is not what we are seeing. We are seeing movement itself, our movement, which we deduce from the fact that a stationary world is pelting past the camera – just as the leaves, pollen, and wings seem to form and reform at terrific speed in Stan Brakhage's *Mothlight* (1963). At times, indeed, our vision seems to go further and we think we are seeing pure film, blank celluloid racing past an aperture, a form of movement, or simulation of movement, that belongs literally to the technology and not to the presented or photographed world.

We can have this feeling as we watch experimental film even when nothing of the kind is happening, precisely because of the sense that the screen and the filmstrip could always close ranks, and the feeling is very strong when the film relies on the relation of a moving camera to a stationary world, as in Brakhage's *Wonder Ring* (1955), a short film mainly shot from the old Third Avenue El train in New York as it goes from station to station – and in that film's brilliant palindromic echo, Joseph Cornell's *Gnir Rednow* (also 1955), the same work flipped from left to right and printed backwards. We see things in these films: stairs, platforms, doors, ticket offices, passengers, office buildings, and warehouses, and some of them occasionally move in their own right. Not all of the film is shot from the moving train either. But the chief and most marvellous effect is that the camera is not catching or representing movement, it is precisely, as in the late scenes in *Entr'acte*, performing movement, making the still world glide by. Gilles Deleuze suggests that 'the mobile camera is like a general equivalent of all the means of locomotion that it shows or makes use of', and Lynne Kirby, also quoted by Mulvey, suggests that early film has a special affinity for trains. We could think that one of our most notable pre-cinematic experiences would be to sit in a train or a car and watch, as we revealingly say, and I have already twice said in this context, the world go by.

This takes us back to my thoughts about movement and animation in the first chapter, which we can now amplify in this way. Invented primarily to capture movement as it really is (or as it really looks), film almost instantly starts playing with different speeds of projection, and with making inert things seem to move of their own accord. The moving camera, whose most durable day job, from the Lumières' factory to yesterday's wedding video, is to keep up with movement in the world, could always turn a travelling shot into sheer travel, a model not a picture of a journey. The pleasure of watching films that evoke these questions – and of thinking about the questions themselves – is the ease with which we do things that sound so difficult conceptually. Without a moment's thought, we separate our perceptions from our understanding: we know what is 'really' moving in a given image, what is 'really' moving but at the wrong speed, and what isn't moving at all – like the apparently approaching wall the hearse in *Entr'acte* seems about to crash into. It's a sort of lesson in relativity. Something is moving here, as nothing is moving in a photograph. But movement is sometimes a fact – a standing person breaks into a trot – and sometimes a relation – this car is moving faster than this camel. And sometimes the relation has to be deduced: the apparent movement of the wall signifies the real movement of the camera. 'Elimination of all fear is in sight', Brakhage writes, and the pun plays out both the opportunity and the abeyance. Knowing what we see, especially when we seem to be seeing something else, can certainly reduce our fear. But then such a possibility is perhaps only 'in sight', on the menu, not within immediate reach or on the table.

The question of what's in sight is also present in experimental works that are apparently much simpler, like Richard Serra's *Hand Catching Lead* (1968) or Marcel Broodthaers' *Rain* (1969). In the first, a hand seen from the side clutches at and tries to catch, sometimes succeeding and sometimes not, small sheets of lead dropped from the top of the frame. The hand adjusts its position within the frame from time to time, and once briefly beckons with a finger at whoever is dropping the lead, suggesting that things need to speed up. But there is no cut and no movement of the camera. The film runs for nearly three minutes. What are we looking at? A bare model of motion, of course, motion captured on camera. Does it matter whether the hand catches the falling lead, and how many times it fails? The title of the film doesn't mention failing at all. No, the point surely is the sight of the clutching hand and the falling lead, grasping and gravity, two sets of motions that meet and miss each other constantly through the film. And – this is perhaps the essential element, the aspect of time that is present within all questions of movement – the film has a duration and everyone gets older as it runs, the owner of the hand, the person tossing the lead, the viewer. Only about three minutes older, to be sure, but the film doesn't want us to forget this, and provides us with a strong visual marker. Whether it catches the lead or misses it, the hand often touches it; at the end of the movie, it is darkened by this contact, the world leaves a dusty leaden trace of its passage, even when the hand, at the end, remains open and empty. To be really exact, the hand is pretty dirty at the beginning, presumably from a dress rehearsal; but it does get darker.

Broodthaers' *Rain* is one of the most haunting of short films. A man, seen from various angles, is sitting in front of a piece of paper spread out on a wooden crate. He has a bottle of ink, dips his pen into it, writes. As he writes, water falls on the page, dilutes the ink, turns the writing into a fluid ink drawing. The man keeps writing; the water keeps falling. Finally, himself soaked, the man gives up. The film lasts a little over two minutes. Its subtitle is 'Project for a text', and its cryptic apparent story suggests failure or poor planning – writing, let's say, is best done indoors, or weather is not kind to script. Its other story, though, the one it enacts rather than tells, is more cheerful: bad timing, writing outdoors when it's raining, gives birth to two new artworks, the inkwashes on the paper and this elegant movie. The first story might be a parable about how easy it can be to defeat chance; and the second story would suggest how little we should want to. There is also a parable about writing and cinema lurking here too, but I'm not sure which way it goes.

But surely these are two instances of movement in the image and not movement of the image? Yes, and we shouldn't confuse the two, even though there are plenty of examples in the cinema of both things happening at once. But the excitement in both cases does arise from movement itself, the collusion of the camera eye and the world in time. When the little girl, right at the end of Louis Malle's *Zazie dans le métro* (1960), is asked what she has done with her weekend in Paris, she says '*J'ai vieilli*', usually (and sensibly) translated as 'I've aged'. She may mean, though, not that she's become old, only that she's become a little older, as everyone in a movie does, and as no one in a photograph can.

Dziga Vertov's *Man with a Movie Camera* (1929) is a great documentary work which is also a strong experimental film, and clearer than most about what its stake is in the cinema. It announces itself as a work that is going to do without title-cards or scenario, and that will owe no allegiance to literature or theatre. It shows us a day in the life of a city – mainly, there are one or two rural excursions – and in its factories and workplaces. It shows a movie-house too, and a (not always rapt) audience. Towards the end of the work, we begin to see more and more of a film – this film – as it is projected to these watchers. We also see the same work, again and again, in the form of numbered filmstrips in an editing room, snipped apart and spliced together. And quite often, we just see the eyes of the editor at work, a sort of metonymy for the translation of sight involved in the making of a film. The editor is Elizaveta Svilova, Vertov's wife, later to become a director in her own right. There are many images superimposed upon others, so that we not only see double but seem to see through each of them, as if neither could quite hold its own against the invasion. There are some startling split-screen effects, especially of traffic, where the image of a tram on the right seems about to collide with an image of the same tram on the left. At times, the planes of the image tilt, so the street or the building seems to arch in on itself. This effect is nowhere more startling than when Moscow's Bolshoi Theatre appears to fall prey to subsidence, each half of the building collapsing towards its centre until the two halves of the roof are vertical and together – a startling image of ruin that is just a rotation of pictures. There is an extraordinarily beautiful little montage of a woman opening a window to let in the morning – she does it only once, but there are four different takes, each from a slightly different angle, and each dissolving gracefully into the next. There are also moments that may recall scenes from *Entr'acte* and certainly anticipate those of *Wonder Ring*. There are many trains; and there is one shot in particular taken from the roof of a moving carriage as it curls away from us round a bend in the tracks: an image of movement and an image in movement.

Everything is quiet at the beginning of the film, quieter than it needs to be for the implied tale of the day in the city's life. People sleep in parks, buses and trains doze in sheds, the machines are all still, shop windows are either shuttered or full of dolls, and the composite animate/inanimate figure is frequent: the unmoving doll in front of the galloping sewing machine, the doll on the bicycle whose stolid face seems to deny the pedalling legs. There is also a moment in the movie-house when the film freezes, so that even the members of the orchestra in the pit – in the pit in the movie within the movie? – are stuck with their bows on their fiddles or their lips at their trombones, until the technician in the cinema sticks two loose pieces of filmstrip together and everything continues perfectly. What all this suggests very strongly is the trope I evoked in my last chapter: the film as the start of life, or a recurring resurrection. This film, like so many others, wants to picture not the invention of film,

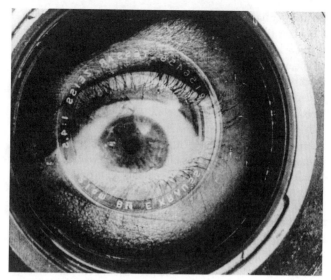

7. Seeing things

but the feeling that invention inspires: that it can 'endow lifeless things with life, or living things with a different kind of life', as Panofsky says.

The title of the movie is very accurate, since the multiple images of our man show him carting his instrument and folded tripod around, scaling towers, perched on top of buildings, clinging to the side of a moving train, chasing ambulances in a car. He is only partly the man shooting a film, since he doesn't need to be in half of these places to shoot anything; he is totally the man with the movie camera, and his travels are a metaphor for everything the camera could possibly see. There are jokes about the metaphor too. At one point, through a superimposition of images, the cameraman and his tripod show up inside a glass of beer. At another, the camera on its tripod (without the man) does a little dance number, coyly bowing its head and stretching its legs like a chorus girl.

Technology has all kinds of unintended lessons. I've seen this film many times, but on my last viewing, when the frames began to freeze after about 23 minutes, my first thought was that the problem was with my computer or the disk, not that this was film art. But the frames freeze systematically, one after the other, until they arrive at a piece of filmstrip, and then whole lines of filmstrip in an editing room. The focus is especially on the faces of several children whom we shall later see, fully animated, at a magic show. This is not quite to say we see photographs and then we see film; we see film waiting to move. Vertov's work is not stuttering or stalling, it's taking us to its heart. What's shocking even now is the life in these children's faces once animated; and the inert composure of the same faces when still. We feel the inertness because we are expecting movement, no doubt; and we get it. But we also begin to sense a whole set of subtle differences where both film and photography have their own forms of force and perfection: between freezing motion and capturing one still moment of it on camera; between static beauty and kinetic promise; between coming to life and going to death. When we say film animates the world, we mean not only that it pictures motion as motion, but that it saves the world from the slowdown or the halt we are always imposing on it. Every frozen frame can find unfrozen life as long as it has other frames for company.

Director's cut

In one sense, the director was always a primary presence in the cinema, whether Fellini and the rest of us knew it or not. Meliès was the trademark of his own films, and if we now think of early German cinema, we are, with some exceptions (*The Golem*, *The Cabinet of Dr Caligari*, both 1920), probably more likely to think of directors' names than film titles: Murnau, Lang, Pabst. There are whole bodies of work we identify with a director's name – Dreyer, Ozu, Bergman, Cocteau – not because they are especially full of the director's personality, but because the name is shorthand for everything the work adds up to, as Virgil, in Jonathan Swift's witty reminder, is taken to mean not 'the person of the famous poet of that name, but only certain sheets of paper, bound up in leather, containing the works of the said poet'.

Still, there were from the early days forces working in the opposite direction: the studio, the producer, and a certain drift towards anonymity that easily takes over popular art. Some films – *Gone with the Wind*, *The Wizard of Oz* (both 1939) – had so many directors they could only be producer or studio works; and if critics regard *Rebecca* (1940) as a Hitchcock film, David O. Selznick and the old public certainly saw it as a Selznick film. The producer indeed is a large part of the fact and the legend of classic American movies. He is the one who builds myths and makes himself larger than life, like Kirk Douglas in *The Bad and the Beautiful* (1952). The director is the man in jodhpurs and flat hat who shouts 'Roll 'em', and 'Cut'. Or in classier versions of the story, he is the man with the German or English accent, the 'artist', but still as fully subordinate to the producer as the writer or the actors are. Whole careers – or at least, whole secondary careers of fable – are made out of the clashes of the director and the producer – Orson Welles and Harry Cohn at Columbia Pictures, let's say – where the romantic genius loses out to crass populism, or if you prefer, the spoiled dreamer meets the man who knows how movies work. It is out of such fables that the equally fabulous notions of *auteur* theory and the director's cut arise.

Auteur theory is standard English for the French phrase '*politique des auteurs*', developed out of the phrase '*cinéma d'auteurs*', first used by François Truffaut in an essay called 'Une certaine tendance du cinéma français'. 'I cannot believe', Truffaut wrote, 'in the peaceful co-existence of the Tradition of Quality [the well-made French films he was attacking, a tradition that he claimed 'despised cinema'] and a cinema of *auteurs*'. '*Auteur*' is intriguingly taken to be untranslatable into English – 'author' obviously won't do – and '*politique*', meaning in context something between a policy and tactic, gets a nice little lift into the slightly more respectable 'theory'. The policy/theory has two main ingredients, one sound but not controversial, the other intuitively appealing and also subversive. The first says what we have already said of certain directors: that their films are their films, artistically signed by them however much help they had. Renoir's films are his own, as are Hitchcock's, although already in a more complicated register, since Hitchcock is working with big-time producers and studios, and much of his art consists in making deals with them and getting things past them. This register points to the second ingredient, and the one French critics and their Anglo followers loved so much: there were secret *auteurs* all over Hollywood, veiled or smothered by the system. The trick was to see them, find their personal touch or quirk wherever it appeared, a nifty individual performance where there might seem to be only an industrial product. Thus Welles could be an *auteur* because we know about his battles with the studio, Hitchcock could be one because he won his battles, but Howard Hawks could be one although we didn't know he had any battles, Curt Siodmak could be one because he was a great technician whose name we had scarcely heard of, and Michael Curtiz, although (because) he was the director of *Casablanca* (1942), would not be an *auteur* at all.

Andrew Sarris asks the essential question. 'How does the *auteur* theory differ from a straightforward theory of directors?' For some, it differs only by its extremism, suggesting that it is 'difficult to think of a bad director making a good film and almost impossible to think of a good director making a bad one' – Sarris is quoting Ian Cameron, who is adapting Truffaut's 'There are no good and bad films, only good and bad directors'. Sarris astutely disavows the extremism – the *auteur* theory has no gift of prophecy, and 'the critic can never assume that a bad director will always make a bad film' – and promptly reinstates its essential effect. 'No, not always, but almost always, and this is the point.' The energy, again, is in the thought of the *auteur*'s identity as achieved against or with a system. Thus, George Cukor 'has a more developed abstract style than...Bergman', and Otto

Preminger is more of an *auteur* than Billy Wilder because he has more 'stylistic consistency'. These are attractive claims even if we think they are wrong, because they invite us to think again about what we are calling art and where we are placing the notion of identity. And yet Sarris's pantheon of *auteurs*, when he lists his top twenty, is pretty much the same as many people's top twenty directors (Sarris's list: Ophuls, Renoir, Mizoguchi, Hitchcock, Chaplin, Ford, Welles, Dreyer, Rossellini, Murnau, Griffith, Sternberg, Eisenstein, von Stroheim, Buñuel, Bresson, Hawks, Lang, Flaherty, Vigo).

Plenty of energy in the idea, then. It emphasizes the director's role generally, draws our attention to talents and styles that may have skilfully disguised themselves as ordinary, and it celebrates mavericks. But there is a certain kind of director the idea characteristically loses or misdescribes. I don't mean the journeyman labourer, although I don't think he should be lost or misdescribed either. I mean the director whose originality lies in eclecticism, whose personal preferences don't have to do with any display of personality at all. It's true that by personality – the second of his three criteria for *auteurship*, the other two are technical mastery and 'interior meaning' – Sarris wants to signal identifiable film style rather than overflowing biography, but the directors I am thinking of are proud of not having a style in this sense. The only figure of this kind on Sarris's list is Howard Hawks, and while critics regularly claim continuities from *Bringing Up Baby* (1937) to *The Big Sleep* (1946) and *Red River* (1948) and from there to *Gentlemen Prefer Blondes* (1953), surely the differences are more interesting. I think also of Louis Malle, who directed within a few years *Les Amants* (1958), *Lift to the Scaffold* (1958), *Zazie* (1960), and *Viva Maria* (1965). And there is Stephen Frears, masterly director of *My Beautiful Laundrette* (1985) and *Dirty Pretty Things* (2002), but also of *Liaisons dangereuses* (1988), *The Grifters* (1990), and *The Queen* (2006). For these men, a certain idea of honour lies in being able to turn one's hand to such different things – and precisely not sign them, as if to refuse the thought that everything had to belong to someone, that it was not enough to do the job well.

It's interesting that Sarris places Mizoguchi so high on his list (after Ophuls and Renoir and before Hitchcock) and doesn't place the masterly Ozu on it at all. I admire Mizoguchi as much as anyone, but would have thought Ozu was the more thoroughly an *auteur*, a great technician whose style is remarkably his own, and who explores similar recesses of mind and society in film after film. Certainly, it's worth pausing over Ozu to see what a director's consistency looks like on film.

Many film-makers create worlds we think we could inhabit, and some of them specialize in this effect, set up whole colonies of the imagination for us. But we can't inhabit the films of Ozu, because he so scrupulously and adamantly situates us as spectators, watchers on the edge of a world we can't enter and can't replicate.

Ozu is famous for the abstemiousness of his style: no flashbacks, and as his career developed, no tracking shots, and not much camera movement of any kind. His images are often taken from very close to the floor, picturing persons who are already placed at a low angle to the world. This camera sits at the end of a corridor in a modern Japanese dwelling. We see into the room at the end, and we know there are rooms to the left and the right. But the geometry seems to be without depth, and quite often the corridor is empty: we are waiting for the inhabitants to show up. The same goes for the city of Tokyo, represented in several films by sheer façades of tall, many-windowed buildings. There must be spaces between them in the form of streets, but we can't see the gaps, because of the camera's head-on, non-perspectival look. The suburban railway station, a favourite location in these movies, feels like a space of extraordinary liberty by comparison. But it too is usually evoked in three static takes, each held for a long minute, and is usually empty, waiting for life. Every now and again, there is a long shot of a hillside covered in trees, or of sand-dunes and the sea: small holidays for the eye, which correspond precisely to the breaks Ozu's characters very occasionally allow themselves from their careers in extravagant modesty.

The films concentrate on families, and on relationships between generations. The characters are so cheerful about what often looks like the desolation of their lives that they might almost become tiresome. Kurosawa, for example, said he didn't like the 'dignified severity' of Ozu's films. He was probably thinking of their austere, self-denying style; but the contents of the films are severely limited too. The characters are not tiresome, though, because the internal spaces of their limited worlds are so vast, and so unforgettably delineated. Consider a famous scene from *Early Summer* (1951). An elderly couple sits in a park, watching children at play. They think of their own son, now married and a father, of their daughter, about to get married, and the father says this is perhaps the happiest time of their life. His wife is not sure. 'Do you think so?' she says. 'We could be happier.' The father doesn't deny this, just says they mustn't want too much. A moment later, we get one of Ozu's rare shots of something other than buildings and people: the open sky, thick clouds almost stationary. A balloon floats upwards, and we watch it for a moment. The next shot shows the couple again. The father, thinking of the balloon, says: 'Some child must be crying.' Now the sky fills the screen again, the balloon a small dot zig-zagging against the clouds. You would think it was an image of freedom if you hadn't been reminded of the crying child.

The characters in Ozu's movies all know they could have been happier. They accept what they've got, but they never lose sight of what they might have had, and that is why we can only watch these films, not inhabit them. To live in an Ozu movie would be to forget too much and remember too much all at once.

David Lynch says he loves the French because they believe in the final cut. They believe, that is, that the director should have the final cut. In most film industries, and especially in Hollywood, someone else – the studio, the producer, the money men – makes the ultimate call on which version of a film to print and distribute. So a director's cut may mean several things: the last version but one of any given film; that same version packaged later for the cinema or for home viewing as an addition or rectification of the first-shown print; and most cynically and commercially, any version of a film at all that is longer than the original release. The romance of the director's war with his unartistic enemies is supposed to do the rest of the work.

The extra material is almost always welcome, rarely changes our view of the film, but there are exceptions. Coppola's *Apocalypse Now Redux* (2001), in spite of its extra fifty minutes or so, does not call itself a director's cut, because Coppola had already cut it once. Some of it is extraordinary, almost a film in its own right, but you can see why Coppola felt it might be distracting. There is a sequence of twenty-five or so restored minutes, in which a group of American soldiers comes across an isolated French plantation, and is invited to a lavish colonial dinner by a family who, apart from being French and settled in the jungle, would be entirely in their element in *The Godfather*. At one point, after a long family discussion of the consequences of Dien Bien Phu (the Army was betrayed by the politicians) and a heated argument about French domestic politics, the host gives an eloquent explanation of why they must stay in this place where they are not wanted, where their time is plainly over. The place is ours, he says, we brought the rubber from Brazil and planted it. 'We want to stay here, captain. We want to stay because it's ours, it belongs to us. I mean, we fought for that. While you Americans are fighting for . . . the biggest nothing in history.' This remark in this context – fine wines, fine linen, old furniture, a child reciting Baudelaire, a man playing an accordion, a venerable grandfather, a spectacular verandah view over the river – offers 'another dimension', as Coppola says. These old-world colonists may be historically in the wrong, but at least they know how to argue against history. When he is asked if he knows about Dien Bien

Phu, the American captain nods sadly. What he is learning is how little he has believed that history needed an argument, and when a French woman asks him if he will go home when the war is over, he says no.

The advertising for an early home video version of the director's cut of *Blade Runner* (1992), by contrast, lays out the whole myth for us impeccably. 'This *is* director Ridley Scott's own version of his sci-fi classic. This version...removes the "uplifting" finale...a great film made greater.' We're certainly better off without the finale, which floats among the clouds and loses us in landscape. It was not so much uplifting as mystifying, offering the audience a chance to forget what it might have just learned, namely that Harrison Ford as well as the woman he loves are not humans but replicants, humanoid robots initially created as slaves for hard labour in 'offworld' colonies. His memories of his early life, his recognition of old photos, all a matter of implants. And more important at this moment, all replicant life has a short expiry date. This helps us towards the creepy everything-is-a-simulation feeling of so much science fiction. But both versions of the film leave us (leave me) more thoroughly haunted by an earlier crisis in the story. Rutger Hauer, as a fierce rebelling replicant, is prepared to save Harrison Ford's life. But Harrison Ford, like the good human he thought he was, had no intention of giving up his job of killing an alien. Fortunately, Hauer's clock has run down. He sits in the rain, remembering what only he can remember, says 'Time...to die', and freezes like a film.

Thinking of the director of a film, and not only of his or her cut, is a way of remembering how much talent and care and hard work goes into any sort of appealing result; and there is a good chance that the director is the mind behind a given film. But sometimes – here is where the notion of the *auteur* is most useful – the writer or the stars provide that mind. Pauline Kael argues persuasively, and without taking anything away from Welles, that Hermann Mankiewicz, the writer, was a major *auteur* of *Citizen Kane*. It's clear that Gene Kelly, Fred Astaire, the Marx Brothers, Buster Keaton, Charlie Chaplin (even when he wasn't directing himself, as he often was) are the chief makers of the films they are in. And sometimes, as I shall suggest in a later section, the genre is the author – the director, writer, actors, cameraman its faithful and ingenious executives.

Drawn to life

In the old days, around 1945, say, when Gene Kelly danced with Jerry the Mouse in *Anchors Aweigh*, encounters between photographed humans and cartoon characters were comic and speedy, and we knew the performers would separate right after their act, go their own ways to distinct ontological regions of the world of entertainment. This is the separation that digital cameras and computer enhancement have made less secure for us, and it's worth recalling that as late as 1988, Robert Zemeckis, in *Who Framed Roger Rabbit?*, could generate funny but also disturbing questions by prolonging the old Kelly scene; that is, by pretending for the length of a whole film that humans and cartoon creatures actually inhabit the same universe, and that both are realities caught by a camera.

In the opening moments, we watch a violent and noisy cartoon, and if we are pretty sure at once that it is not the real Disney or Warner Brothers thing, it is because it is so parodically hectic, even by their standards. We are still not prepared, however, to hear a director shout 'Cut', and see the cartoon character, a rotund baby, walk off the set and talk like an ageing comedian, complete with cigar in his mouth. He says he'll be in his trailer waiting for the next take, and in one magical move he crosses from the flat, high-coloured drawn world of the film in which he stars to the apparently three-dimensional space he and everyone else in the movie lives in. The moment when his graphic hand flips the skirt of a 'real' assistant makes us think not of a neat occasional trick of two representational technologies but of some incomprehensible clash of worlds, as when a character in a novel, for example, or a

Woody Allen film, claims a materiality and a history unpartitioned from ours.

The cartoon characters in the film, although they share a continuous habitat with the humans, live in a separate part of the city and are generally regarded as predictable stereotypes – which indeed they are, since they began life on a drawing board and not in biology. The film doesn't question the accuracy of the stereotypes, indeed it reinforces them in the end by making its villain a cartoon figure disguised as a human, or at least as Christopher Lloyd. But it does ask how stereotypes get made in general, and who makes them; and its whole racial allegory – the so-called 'toons' in this film strongly resemble the cheerily amenable or anarchic, ineffably alien African Americans in old Hollywood movies – pleads for a tolerance of modes of life different from what we take to be the mainstream.

At one point, Jessica Rabbit, Roger's wife, a slinky humanoid cartoon figure, all curves and emphatic sex appeal, a sort of permanent night-club hostess, says winsomely, 'I'm not bad. I'm just drawn like that.' Her voice and figure make the statement a little hard to believe, but her logic is impeccable. She didn't draw herself, she is the product of someone else's graphic gift, along with his or her prejudices or desires.

And at an even more startling criss-crossing moment in the film, the actor Bob Hoskins finds himself handcuffed to the cartoon Roger Rabbit. Roger has thrown away the key to the cuffs, which for some time causes all kinds of comic turbulence for the attached couple. Finally, Roger just wriggles his hand and easily frees himself. Hoskins is outraged, and says, 'You mean you could have done that at any time?' Roger, stung by the accusation, seems genuinely surprised at having to explain the rules of his world. 'Not at any time', he says emphatically. 'Only when it was funny.' When the apparent bondage had got enough laughs, that is, and when the escape would provoke laughter for a different reason.

The history of animation is often very well told as a flight into realism, a decline from the pointed abstraction of awkward figures like Little Lulu, Felix the Cat, and even the early Mickey Mouse, into the conventional all-American graces of Snow White and Cinderella. Walt Disney, the argument goes, became so enamoured of verisimilitude that he invested all his fantasies in it, and finally built his cartoons as real estate. This is certainly part of the story, but there is also travel in the opposite direction, especially when we think of the influence of Japanese manga comics and the stylistically related anime films on recent Disney Studio work – all those huge-eyed heroes and heroines who go back to *Remi* (1977) and *Akira* (1989) and continue into *Mulan* (1998) – and of the very different visual styles of Pixar films. The interesting question is what animated films in the literal sense are doing that photomechanical films, to use Sean Cubitt's term, can't do.

I know the question is traditionally put the other way round, and often very eloquently – by Stanley Cavell and Dudley Andrew, among others. And it is not enough of an answer to say that there are plenty of resemblances between the two modes of film, that they even quite often obey the same narrative laws. There are plenty of moments in photography-based film where things happen only when they're funny – think of the timing of Joe E. Brown's remark at the end of *Some Like It Hot* (1959) when he learns that the girl he wants to marry is a boy: 'Nobody's perfect'. But then think of what it would take to turn the Jack Lemmon character into a girl – a biological girl, that is, and not the woman he is pretending to be. In life, it would require serious surgery, and in the movie it would require new casting and new production. Cartoons are like writing in this sense: they need only a movement of a pen to alter a world. And if the distinction between photography and cartoon is pitched as an opposition between the attempt to capture the real and sheer indulgence in the manipulation of it, we have to pause over the attempt. 'The cinema's ultimate aim', Bazin wrote, 'should not be so much to mean as to reveal'. The same (rather loaded) distinction may, as I have suggested, make us worry about digital work on film. 'The films some of us most care about', Dudley Andrew says, carefully glossing Bazin's proposition, 'aim to discover, to encounter, to confront, and to reveal'. Digital work can do this too, of course, and photographed films don't have to, as the old myth had it. But there is a resistance in photography ('Cinema confronts us with something resistant', in Andrew's words, 'but not necessarily with the solid body of the world') that graphic art has to work much harder to find.

Still, I doubt whether any photographed face offers more grainy resistance to simple interpretation than a Rembrandt self-portrait. And Stanley Cavell, defending his 'assumption ... that cartoons are not movies' because they are not 'projections of the real world', offers some extraordinary insights into what cartoons are. Their creatures give in to gravity, for example, not when their weight compels them to, but when they become aware of it. And then: 'Their bodies are indestructible, one might almost say immortal.' 'Cartoon violence can be funny because while it is very brutal it cannot be bloody.' Finally, 'Cartoon terror is absolute, because since the body is indestructible, the threat is to the soul itself.' These hardly sound like the elements of a minor art-form, or evasions of reality.

If we put these notations alongside the moments I've described in *Who Framed Roger Rabbit?* – the presumption of one world where we thought there were two, the subordination of moral character to a prior design, a law of laughter that works like the law of gravity in our physics – we see a small fraction of what makes cartoons so durable. Their characters are either pure mind or pure soul. They fall only when they remember gravity, they never die, they can't bleed, they are condemned to a life of making us laugh, and their terror, when it strikes them, is absolute. They are what we are not, they are the opposite of everything documentary cinema reminds us that we are and have been; and they are also, of course, on another frequency, as Ralph

Ellison's invisible man would say, versions of ourselves both as liberated from the flesh and imprisoned in the poverty of fantasy. A great deal of, perhaps most, written and oral fiction is like this, hence all the genies and monsters and vamps we find in narratives from the *Odyssey* to the *Arabian Nights* to *Dracula*. Realism, whatever its instrument, is an honourable refusal of such excursions, a loyalty to the stubborn, unarranged matter of human life; but the excursions are not only evasions. They too have realities – of anxiety and desire and hope, among many other candidates – to explore.

A brilliant exploration of this kind takes place in the anime film *Ghost in the Shell*, directed by Manoru Oshii (1995, with a sequel in 2004). Here is a world partly derived from Ridley Scott's *Blade Runner*, and partly, in its Jessica Rabbit mode, from *Playboy* – the visual interest in the female cyborg's splendid naked breasts may strike some as a little obsessive. The time is the future, the city is that strange cross of Tokyo and Los Angeles that everyone assumes will take over our tomorrow, and the plot concerns the infiltration of a state security system by a hacker called the Puppetmaster. There are sinister figures in the Foreign Office who may be for or against Section 9, the security outfit, and even the humans in the story have so many mechanical spare parts that they are a little unsure of what distinguishes them from robots. The robots, meanwhile, or at least the more thoughtful of them, know that nothing distinguishes them from humans except their own troubled consciousness, and Kusanagi, also known as the Major, given to citing St Paul's Epistle to the Corinthians ('For now we see through a glass, darkly; but then face to face: now I know in part; but then shall I know even as also I am known', although it doesn't sound all that much like this in the American soundtrack), wants not only to combat the Puppetmaster, which is her job since she works for Section 9, but to find out what makes him tick, or in her language to have a conversation with his ghost. After a violent and dramatically drawn – and drawn-out – battle, she gets her wish, and the

8. Now what would a human do?

Puppetmaster proposes a kind of marriage of spirits. They merge technologically, with lots of whirring messages, and both begin to inhabit her new (still female but now rather girlish) body – the old Playboy-derived one got badly smashed up in the battle. The sequel continues the story.

Kusanagi has a thick mop of black hair, dark eyes, and the schematic features of a comic-book boy – plus the ultra-female body I've already mentioned. She is not drawn from reality but from a complication of fear and desire, just like the urban landscape she inhabits. Her physical features, like the city's skyscrapers, alleys, canals, and glittering electronic advertisements, resemble those of a biology and a world we half-know, but they are finally only helpless allusions to them. They don't resemble a conception of those things because they *are* a conception of them, lavishly pictured. The pathos of the thought that neither Kusanagi nor her city can achieve even the secondary reality of a photograph is considerable, and we may think for comparison of the cloned child in Steven Spielberg's *A.I.* (2001). Here, we are invited to feel deep sympathy for a non-human creature, to respect its longing to be one of us, and are substantially helped out by the fact that the artificial child is represented by a photographed actual person, not a computer-generated creature or a drawing. Kusanagi is not only 'drawn like that', as Jessica Rabbit is, she is something like an incarnation of drawing itself, the picture of a picture who wonders if she will ever be anything else.

Anime films cover all kinds of topics, and often do nothing but delight in the power and freedom of graphic art. In *Akira*, for example, an injured electronic arm becomes an oceanic monster, a writhing Leviathan ready to devour the world, and the mood of the film reflects nothing but horror-movie exuberance, very similar to that of many live-action films with lots of help from computers. But *The Ghost in the Shell* suggests a genuine graphic melancholy, a counterpart to the old myth of the inability of photography *not* to capture reality. The dream here would be of escape not into the imagination but out of it, of delivery from the highly stylized life forms of panic and prejudice figured as entertainment.

Chapter 3
The colour of money

Art and industry

Film began as a very small business, a dramatic invention but a tiny piece of the world of entertainment. It was an act among others in a variety show. Very soon, though, there were shows composed only of films, and there were special places for their showing. A cinema called the Nickelodeon opened in Pittsburgh in 1905, and by 1907 there were 4,000 such places in the United States. Something resembling an industry developed in France, Italy, England, and Germany too, and audiences grew and grew across the world. Studios were born: Pathé and Gaumont in France; UFA in Germany; Universal, Twentieth Century Fox, and Paramount in the USA. Hollywood itself, a small California town surrounded by orange groves, became a movie settlement because of its steady weather (and because California was thought to be far enough away from the lawsuits that rained down on experimenters and investors in New York). Something like the contours of later patterns of film-making began to form. Stars began to glitter. And above all, money began to gleam.

A whole support system blossomed: publicity machinery, fan magazines, prizes, record-keeping. Box-office results became the equivalent of sporting scores, or world championship boxing.

Avatar (2009) is the largest grossing picture ever made, unless we adjust for inflation, in which case the title goes to *Gone with the Wind* (1939), and *Avatar* moves to fourteenth place. The American Academy of Motion Pictures awarded its first Oscars in 1929, and has awarded them every year since. Programmes developed from sets of short films to single feature films plus supporting entries; and from there to the two film diet that was standard fare for so long. By 1929, 90 million cinema tickets were sold each week in America, with figures proportionally similar elsewhere. There were ups and downs during the Depression and the Second World War, but the figure had reached one hundred million by 1946. By 1955, however, the number was down to 46 million, not a whole lot more than the 40 million or so of 1922. Movie-houses, of which a little more later, rose and fell, naturally enough, to the same rhythm: there were 20,000 in America in 1947 and 11,000 in 1959.

Programmes often changed midweek, and shows were continuous, so you could come in at the middle of a film and stay till you got the middle again. Hence the now almost unintelligible phrase 'This is where we came in'. There is a remarkable piece by the humorist Robert Benchley about a game he liked to play. Arriving, say, twenty minutes into a film, he would give himself five minutes to reconstruct the plot so far. Then he would interpret everything that followed in the light of his reconstruction. He would stay on to see how close he was – or pretend to see. He claimed many movies were improved by his method.

Theories of the Seventh Art arose, as well as plenty of attacks on the mindlessness of moviegoers. It was in reaction to one such attack that Walter Benjamin developed an important piece of the argument of his essay 'The Work of Art in the Age of its Technological Reproducibility' (various versions between 1935 and 1939). The French novelist Georges Duhamel had included an onslaught on cinema in his witty and gloomy book on America, *Scènes de la vie future* (1930). The relevant chapter is titled 'cinematographic interlude or the entertainment of the free citizen', and within the text, the cinema is called, in the same mode of grand irony, a sanctuary, a temple, an abyss of forgetfulness, and the cave of the monster. Duhamel says that film 'requires no kind of effort' and 'presupposes no capacity for consecutive thought', *aucune suite dans les idées*. Benjamin agrees that film audiences are distracted but claims that there are forms of distraction that may function as localized, medium-specific attention. 'Even the distracted person', he says, thinking of the moviegoer, 'can form habits'. 'The audience', he adds, 'is an examiner, but a distracted one'.

Duhamel, Benjamin implies, dislikes the cinema because he dislikes the masses. We don't have to like what the masses like – unless, of course, 'we' are the masses. Even Benjamin is prepared to speak of the 'disreputable form' of some popular entertainment. But we do have to see that the world changes, and that quantity doesn't necessarily ruin quality.

This argument is still running and looks forward to a discussion of genre I shall take up later. For many scholars, and for middle-brow audiences, genres can provide art only if they are transformed or publicly abandoned, redeemed from commerce and vulgarity by irony. Selected Hollywood items thus slip into the category of art-house cinema, and are saved. Such viewers answer attacks on the movies not by becoming distracted examiners but by showing how the movies allow them to concentrate. Clint Eastwood's magnificent *The Outlaw Josey Wales* (1976), for example, would no longer be a western but a 'western'; an intelligent parody of a mode in itself rather stupid.

My sense of these things is almost exactly the opposite. When a bounty-hunter, in that same movie, tells Eastwood that he is 'wanted', our hero says, in a drawl borrowed from fifty years' worth of supposedly laconic movie westerners, 'Reckon I'm right popular'. Defending his trade as a bounty-hunter, this person says,

'A man's got to do something for a living these days', provoking in Eastwood the impeccable understatement, 'Dyin' ain't much of a living, boy'. Soon after this, Eastwood kills his pursuer, taking the argument beyond words. These are great lines and action, but they are not moments of parody, this is a straight western. *The Outlaw Josey Wales* is better than most films in the genre, but not because it does something different. It does the same thing better, and the quiet knowingness of moments like the ones I have just described is not irony. It is the voice of genre doing what genre does. The distracted examiner might give the same marks as the concentrating one, but for different reasons.

The large point is that entertainment doesn't have to be rescued from itself to become art; and that it may not be any better at all for being thought of as art. It is striking that when Peter Wollen, as serious a theorist and film-maker as one could wish to encounter, lists his preferences for us, they include Disney as well as Kurosawa, and von Sternberg as well as Michael Snow and Hollis Frampton. Art and industry may be at odds, and they are certainly not the same thing. But we have everything to gain from thinking of them together.

Moviegoers

In the beginning, the movies were working-class entertainment, a little too rough and ready for the middle classes. But various social groups soon merged into a single capacious audience, and the cinemas became posher and posher. An important distinction remained, though, between film and theatre – or between a whole range of popular arts, on the one hand, and the more exclusive, selective experience of seeing a play, for instance. It was not about class but about focus. For a large part of the 20th century, people went to see movies, not a movie; they saw whatever was on the bill, and many of them went twice or more a week. The idea of buying a ticket for a particular performance, as we do now, and of buying a ticket which entitles you to a particular seat in the auditorium, was alien to most film audiences until the 1960s. Not completely alien, of course, at least in spirit. There were films that people who rarely went to the cinema felt they had to see. There were huge hits and sad flops. But the central habit remained: moviegoers were moviegoers.

Of course, it's a habit to go to the cinema once a week to see a film you've picked out from the newspapers and reserved your seats for online, but it's not the same kind of habit. There was a saturation represented in the old moviegoing, offering an extraordinary intensity of film reference one could pick up without concentrating, while merely (merely) enjoying oneself. This surely is what Benjamin means when he speaks of the audience as a distracted examiner. This examiner is a genuine expert, no doubt about it, can read the slightest change of expression on a favourite star's face, knows exactly when the suave villain is going to turn nasty, and is always sure the heroine will overcome her tears and find her inner strength when she needs to. The charm is that this examiner would never *think* of herself as an expert – at best as fan, but she might also be a little more disinterested than that, she might simply feel that the movies were a kind of imaginative home, that she knew all the corners of that world, that it couldn't surprise her except in ways that were part of a design she understood. This is a precious kind of knowledge, and only some sort of saturation will provide it.

The saturation in several countries was guaranteed not only by prolific national film production and a good deal of exporting and importing, but by a system that was the life of the studio – so much so that when it ended, the studios in their old form ended too. The system was what came to be broken up as a monopoly: the companies that made the films also owned the cinemas, they didn't have to sell the films to anyone, only ship them out to their own franchises. This doesn't seem to leave audiences much choice – but they had a lot of films not to choose from, and of course, they didn't know about the choices they didn't have.

We don't have to romanticize (or despise) this kind of moviegoing, but many arguments about film are based on a relation or non-relation to it. Critics claim to have been in what Lawrence Alloway calls 'the target zone' – they were addicted viewers before they became cool judges. Or they claim to have had quite a different connection to the cinema from the start. Pauline Kael, for example, loved the movies but thought 'the cinema' was a dangerous abstraction, the looming death-threat of the idea of art. 'If we've grown up at the movies,' she wrote, 'we know that good work is continuous not with the academic, respectable tradition but with the glimpses of something good in trash'. Alert moviegoing means distrusting all claims of art and (if absolutely necessary) finding flickers of art in works where no claims are being made. This angle is quite different from that of what Susan Sontag, in a famous article, calls 'cinephilia'. Cinephilia is falling in love with the cinema rather than the movies, and you love what it can do at its best; you don't have to feel bad about its being art.

But cinephilia could include moviegoing, as Sontag makes clear:

> Until the advent of television emptied the movie theaters, it was from a weekly visit to the cinema that you learned (or tried to learn) how to walk, to smoke, to kiss, to fight, to grieve. Movies gave you tips about how to be attractive. Example: It looks good to wear a raincoat even when it isn't raining. But whatever you took home was only a part of the larger experience of submerging yourself in lives that were not yours.... You wanted to be kidnapped by the movie. To be kidnapped, you have to be in a movie theater, seated in the dark among anonymous strangers.

All kinds of things have happened to film audiences since the last days of the old moviegoing, but mainly, in so far as they are still film audiences at all – that is, sitting together in a cinema in the dark – they have grown incredibly young. This explains the existence of a great many movies, which represent brash bids for a piece of this market; but leaves us at a loss to account for all the films that can't be aimed at this audience and nevertheless do well financially. And of course, these youngsters don't award prizes or Oscars. Film critics gesture towards the audience's youth when they're stuck for something to say, but otherwise seem to get on very well by ignoring it. Meanwhile, though, something else has happened, and has been happening since the 1970s. The cinema is not the only place to see a film, and it is no longer the place where most films are seen.

The rise and fall of the picture palace

They are boarded up now; have become revivalist churches or bingo halls; or have vanished entirely. If they're still cinemas, they are split into small boxes with separate screens. *Variety* cheerfully reported that in 1990 there were 23,689 screens in the United States – but very few of them were in single theatres. Yet not too long ago, certainly all the way through the 1950s and 1960s, even relatively small towns in England and America had their six or seven one-screen cinemas each, with their exotic names and fanciful architecture. They were called (in Lincoln, where I grew up) The Grand, The Central, The Savoy, The Regal, The Ritz, and the Radion, and they had similar names everywhere, glancing at fancy hotels and the high life. In Los Angeles, they were, and still are, called The Orpheus, The Rialto, The Tower, The Globe, The Arcade, The Cameo, The Roxie – and that's just one side of one street.

Inside, they looked like opera houses or ballrooms, or even grander or more exotic locations, with masses of gold leaf all over the walls and the ceilings; but they also often had an Art Deco look, and they went in for a lot of coloured lighting, reds, greens, and blues. Here's part of a report on the Capitol Theater in Chicago in 1925:

> The auditorium…might be briefly described as representing an Italian garden under a Mediterranean sky, featuring a moonlit night. On the left side of the auditorium is an Italian palace façade.

The right side of the auditorium represents a terraced roof garden with a small temple building. Surmounting the whole is a representation of deep blue sky with moving clouds and twinkling stars, creating a completely out-of-door setting.

Long after sound had taken over the cinema, these places quite frequently had organs, and the real excitement was not the recital of show tunes that preceded any given screening, but the sight of the organ, glittering like a fairground, rising up out of nowhere, the organist already blasting away; and sinking into darkness again as the recital ended. Sheer magic, and part of what the movies used to mean: they were the native creatures of this strange place, we were the visitors, trailing all the dust and fret and memories of waking life.

There are wonderful, melancholy studies of the lives of these buildings, their architects, their publics, their neighbourhoods. And it is, in a sense, only now that we can see how grand and complicated the cultural assertion was that they were engaged in. For example, all that glitz and glamour didn't always introduce *The Wizard of Oz*; it introduced stark dramas in black and white, and until the late 1950s, in most places there was a newsreel, full of invasive images of actual, marching life, and complete with one of those (always male) voices that seemed to guarantee truthfulness through its never-failing bossy cadences and rhythms. Even *The Wizard of Oz* would be a documentary if one of these men narrated it.

Films like *Mulholland Drive* (2001) and *Blade Runner* (1982) revisit and remythify these magical places (both use former movie-houses as significant locations) but in a rather forlorn way, as Stephen Barber says in his book on old cinemas in Los Angeles and what came to be shown in them: image after image of death, erasure, and the end of film itself. 'Film's end', indeed, is Barber's recurring, dramatic name for whatever is happening to film, which he also pictures as its transformation, its mutation, or its absorption into a sort of digital portfolio of options. He also shows

9. Coming soon and soon going

'how film images ... appeared complicit with their own decay and downfall' even before there was any decay and downfall in the offing. Did these extravagant palaces generate dreams of their own and everyone's ruin?

No, but moviegoers always knew these buildings were a bribe as well as a fantasy, that darkness and death lived in the films alongside all the frolics and the happy endings, that the gleaming unrealities of the architecture could never be the whole story. We took the style of the place and the mood of the film for what they were: not everything had to match or make sense. We didn't think the organ playing inflected the news, and we didn't think either of them affected our friends out on a date in the back row.

But just consider this occasion. The year is 1948, and the pupils at all four grammar schools in our town – and no doubt in lots of other towns, this was part of a whole drive to show cinema was culture in Britain – are being taken to the movies instead of going to classes. Two thousand children pile into The Ritz to see Olivier's *Hamlet*. Is it possible that all this educational earnestness didn't alter The Ritz for us? Is it possible that The Ritz didn't do something for *Hamlet*, make it more of a movie than it would have been in an arts cinema, for example? We know now, of course, that it was very much a movie, including a near-suicide scene complete with ocean that Laurence Olivier had borrowed from Hitchcock's *Rebecca* (1940), in which he had starred. But at the time, it was sold to us as pure culture, the only way most of us were going to see Shakespeare except by being in (or being dragged to) the school play. We believed this, but The Ritz and its neon lighting were whispering something else to us, something that perhaps these movie palaces often murmured to audiences around the world. They said they couldn't actually promise magic and mystery and grandeur, couldn't live up to all the lurid messages of their architecture; but even so, they would never let us down, because they would never leave anything as it was, whether it was the news or *Hamlet* or *Flash Gordon*. The very slightness of the change might be part of the attraction. We wouldn't know why the world was different in there; just that it was. Even as late as 2005, the philosopher Jacques Rancière could picture the movie-house as a combination of a dreaming child's bedroom and a lost museum.

One more time

The concept of genre is much older than the movies, of course, and is a crucial aspect of the study of painting, literature, and music. But film probably *likes* genre more than any other form or medium does now. It's as if the pleasures of repetition, recognition, variation, renewal were an essential part of what film does and what filmgoers like to see.

Many, perhaps most, post-romantic works of high culture pretend we have never seen or heard anything like them before: originality and difference are their dream and definition. Conversely, all genre works in any medium assume we have grown up on their likes, and imaginatively can never have known a first one. To read an epic poem, or to watch a western, is to have in mind a cloud of antecedents and parallels, none of them necessarily looking like anything as direct as an allusion, but all of them at work *as a cloud*, the feel of the genre itself: all the titanic battles and athletic competitions we half-remember, all the gunfights we have ever seen. We may even have made some of them up, like a composite portrait, but they will still be part of what a genre is, the backdrop against which any new instance will play. Franz Kafka evokes a remark we recall from 'a nebulous bunch of old stories, although it may not occur in any of them'. A wonderful thought. A genre begins the moment such a memory – or fiction of such a memory – can arise. Philip Larkin gets this effect very well in his poem 'The Poetry of Departures':

Sometimes you hear, fifth-hand,
As epitaph:

> *He chucked up everything*
> *And just cleared off,*
> And always the voice will sound
> Certain you approve
> This audacious, purifying,
> Elemental move.

We don't even have to hear the phrase 'fifth-hand': we've always already heard it, just as somewhere among our self-deceptions we have espoused the fake freedom signalled in the words 'audacious', 'purifying', and 'elemental'. Only stay-at-homes talk like this. The rest have left.

There are many kinds of film genres and subgenres (comedy, screwball comedy, black comedy, Ealing comedy, comedy-thriller, and so on), and just starting to name them can make you sound like Polonius. But they all have a good deal in common – enough for us to compare them, and to see where the significant differences among them start. I'm going to look at three long-running and stalwart genres – the western, the musical, and the gangster film – and then briefly at one almost-genre I've made up, which I'm calling the 'old friend'.

The first movie western was Edwin S. Porter's *The Great Train Robbery* (1903), and literally thousands followed in the next decades. The great name here is that of the director John Ford, although Howard Hawks and others made fine westerns. A very partial list of significant works would include: *The Covered Wagon* (James Cruze, 1923), *The Iron Horse* (John Ford, 1924), *Stagecoach* (John Ford, 1939), *Red River* (Howard Hawks, 1948), *The Gunfighter* (Henry King, 1950), *Winchester 73* (Anthony Mann, 1950), *High Noon* (Fred Zinnemann, 1952), *Shane* (George Stevens, 1953), *The Man from Laramie* (Anthony Mann, 1955), *The Searchers* (John Ford, 1956), *Rio Bravo* (Howard Hawks, 1959), *The Man Who Shot Liberty Valance* (John Ford, 1962), *The Magnificent Seven* (John Sturges, 1960), *The Wild Bunch* (Sam Peckinpah, 1969).

By the time of the last film on the list, the genre had taken a new, apparently quite different, direction in the form of the so-called 'spaghetti westerns', directed most notably by Sergio Leone (*A Fistful of Dollars*, 1964; *For a Few Dollars More*, 1965; *The Good, the Bad and the Ugly*, 1966). These were Italian films shot largely in Spain, and were at first thought to be enjoyable spoofs, European riffs in a film language only North Americans could speak properly. But they weren't spoofs, any more than Jean-Luc Godard's *Breathless* (1960) was a spoof of an American gangster movie. They were stylized acts of homage that entered and changed the genre. No film historian now would *not* count them as westerns, and they had, in any case, one remarkable pay-off in the notional homeland: the westerns of Clint Eastwood, who had emerged from television to star in the Leone films, and who as actor and director brought magnificent new life to the old preoccupations of the genre. Orson Welles claimed that if anyone but Eastwood had made *The Outlaw Josey Wales*, it would have been called a classic, and by the time Eastwood made *Unforgiven* (1992), people were beginning to say everything he did was a classic.

There were many cross-overs, and sometimes the west began in Japan. *The Magnificent Seven* is a version of Kurosawa's *Seven Samurai* (1954), and *A Fistful of Dollars* is based on Kurosawa's *Yojimbo* (1961). Does any of this suggest that the western is not an American genre? Not exactly. It does remind us, as philosophers and politicians from Emerson to Obama keep saying, that America is not a place, or not only a place. It is an idea of a place, and the mythical west is one of its most developed regions. The time there is always on the edge of history, society is about to be formed, the law about to settle into place, the railroad promised, the Civil War recently over. If you have cattle, someone will steal them; if you have a house, someone will burn it. There may be a sheriff or a marshal, a good man perhaps, but a weak one; or a man in the pay of the bad guys, who congregate in this region as if it were just made for them – as indeed, in terms of narrative, it is.

How could there be shoot-ups if there was no one to do the shooting?

With any luck, a homeless gunfighter will ride into town, take the side of virtue, kill off the villains, and move on. He can't stay, because he is tainted by the violence he has used to overcome violence – there is more than a hint of very ancient rituals here. Quite often, the law is precariously preserved because a criminal gets taken by train to a city closer to civilization (as in *3.10 to Yuma*, 1957), or is kept in prison against all odds until the visiting judge can arrive (as in *Rio Bravo*). The man who shot Liberty Valance, in the title of this great movie, is James Stewart, now a United States Senator, a representative of the victory of law over the old lawlessness. That is, he is the man who faced Liberty Valance and tried to shoot him. The man who actually shot Liberty Valance was John Wayne, a decent representative of the old lawless days, and now dead, the familiar lonely scapegoat for violence, his code of honour broken by his having to shoot a man from the side in order to save another man's life. The frame narrative of the movie has James Stewart telling this old history to a journalist, who follows it all eagerly, but is not going to write any of it up. 'When the legend becomes fact', he says, 'print the legend'. 'America' becomes doubly mythological here: home of the secret truth, known to a few locals and millions of moviegoers, and a realm of legend, where the truth is always what it is supposed to be. It's striking, as Fenin and Everson say in their book on westerns, how often the law itself is corrupt in westerns, part of the problem not the solution; but this is really the counterpart of the stories I've just evoked: remote, delayed, feeble, or broken, the law is a persistent, troubled preoccupation.

Westerns come and go, and rumours of the death of the genre have been frequent, and sometimes even plausible. There were times, watching *Silverado* (Laurence Kasdan, 1985), say, or *Dances with Wolves* (Kevin Costner, 1990), when our enjoyment itself was sorrowful. *Silverado*, especially, felt like a brilliant guidebook to the genre rather than an example of it. These friendly events weren't movies so much as acts of mourning for a kind of film no one could make any more. Except that someone could; did; will. Instances are Jim Jarmusch's *Dead Man* (1996); Tommy Lee Jones', *The Three Burials of Melquiades Estrada* (2005); James Mangold's remake of *3.10 to Yuma* (2007).

The history of musicals is not like this. There are great names and great periods, there are spells of seeming silence, and the genre is so capacious that we may wonder whether it is a genre at all. *Carmen Jones* (1954) and *Porgy and Bess* (1959), for example, are brilliant musical works, but we are likely to think of them as filmed operas rather than film musicals. Similarly, we probably see the operettas of the 1930s as just that: operettas. Even if we accept these borders, though, there is still a large distance from a Fred Astaire movie to *Rock Around the Clock* (1956) or *Saturday Night Fever* (1977); and Carol Reed's wonderful *Oliver* (1968) is very different again.

We could separate musicals that began life as movies from those that were recreated on film after their success on the stage. The former group would contain masterpieces like *An American in Paris* (1951), *Singin' in the Rain* (1952), and *All That Jazz* (1978), and would allow us to think about the energy and invention released by the medium, as distinct from the rather stately, stagey reproductions represented by films like *My Fair Lady* (1964), *Kiss Me Kate* (1953), *South Pacific* (1958), or even *Guys and Dolls* (1955). But then, *On the Town* (1949), a great Broadway success, is filmed in such a way as to make it feel like a movie original, making amazing use of New York City streets and buildings and docks. Whatever we think, we need a way of paying attention to *A Hard Day's Night* (1964) without losing sight of *Sweeney Todd* (2007). But then, isn't the stretch too much; is there anything to be said about such a sweep of works taken together?

Musicals are about sight as well as sound, about spectacle and filling the screen, and the elaborate films of Busby Berkeley, beginning with his dance creations in *42nd Street* and *Golddiggers of 1933* (both 1933), and continuing into works he directed like *Ziegfeld Girl* and *Babes on Broadway* (both 1941), are already as elaborate as anything to follow. For a moment, it looked as if the genre might settle into a version of flower-arrangement, all chorus girls in intricate clusters and caught in repeated high-angle shots. But fortunately, two other things had already happened. The genre had developed its favourite story line and Fred Astaire had arrived.

The story line involved putting on a show in the course of the film, getting one's act together in the most literal and the most fulsomely metaphorical senses. The kids – Mickey Rooney and Judy Garland, say – have to work to get their talents known and their friends organized, and this need provides both the story line and the triumphant last scene – although the supposed practice routines are pretty professional too, we are at the movies, not really in the village barn. This is the plot of *Babes in Arms* (1939), for example, and it was still going strong, although in a very sophisticated fashion and with rather more senior characters, in Vincente Minnelli's *The Bandwagon* (1953).

The Fred Astaire story was different. There were often floor shows in the plots of his films, and he danced in them, but the cue for music was not a show business ambition – Astaire always seemed beyond ambition, sheltered from such uncertainties in a realm of poise and irony – but an artistic game or a need of expression. His numbers with Ginger Rogers in films like *Top Hat* (1935), *Swing Time* (1936), and *Shall We Dance* (1937) are literally forms of courtship through grace and skill, the physical equivalent of the verbal battles and truces of Cary Grant and Irene Dunne or Spencer Tracy and Katharine Hepburn in screwball comedy. These people belong together not because they like each other or because the script says so, but because they are visibly made for each other – because neither has any imaginable equal except the other. This is what one song calls 'la belle, la perfectly swell romance', but it's a very special romance: all wit and performance, no sentiment in sight, or at least no mere sentiment.

Gene Kelly is not really Astaire's heir or rival, but it is hard not to think of them together because of the way they magnetized the elements of the films they were in, concentrated sound and story into tales and meanings and images that belonged only to them – whoever was directing them, and whoever had written the material. That said, the differences are what matter. Astaire's *tours de force* were astonishing tap solos, feats of singing that appeared not to be singing at all, just a form of talking that happened to be in tune, and his swooping, swinging, impeccably synchronized dances with (ideally) Ginger Rogers. Life in this image was fast, elegant, funny, and a little risky, you could always miss the beat or lose your balance. But you didn't.

Kelly performed some amazing dances with Vera-Ellen, Leslie Caron, Cyd Charisse, and others; but our lasting image is of him either alone – in the title number of *Singin' in the Rain*, in its fantastic retake on roller-skates in *It's Always Fair Weather* – or engaging with children and policemen and curious passers-by. His singing is a little closer to conventional crooning than Astaire's is, but it is similarly without operatic ambitions. His dancing, however, not only keeps edging toward the ballet within the story that became fashionable for a while, it keeps athletically reinventing modern dance at it goes. Astaire, we might say, experiments in order to become more classical. Kelly experiments to remake the medium. As Peter Wollen reminds us in his excellent little book on *Singin' in the Rain*, Kelly has the support of a strong technical and musical unit at MGM, but he was always at the front of the film, literally and imaginatively, and was constantly thinking of new ways not only to dance but to dance on film.

There is an elegant homage to his success in this mode in Jacques Demy's two musicals, *Les Parapluies de Cherbourg*

(1964) and *Les Demoiselles de Rochefort* (1969). Set, as their names suggest, in real French ports, they are shot in high colour and costume as if the French provinces were just a Hollywood lot with people and cars passing through it. We may think of several earlier movies as we watch these late, artful (and yes, a bit sentimental) works, and it won't matter greatly which we think of (just nebulous old stories), but the odds are they'll be Gene Kelly movies anyway. In the second of the Demy movies, Kelly appears himself, playing an American composer looking for an old friend in Rochefort. He falls in love with Françoise Dorléac, who plays the sister of her real-life sister Catherine Deneuve (*'Nous sommes des soeurs jumelles/Nées sous le signe des jumeaux'*, is their opening song), and at one point is given a bravura spot, which glances at his version of 'I got rhythm' in *An American in Paris* – French children appear here too and briefly interact with Kelly – and is also an agile and original piece in its own right. A slow, rather balletic opening gives way to a fast jazz beat (music by Michael Legrand) and suddenly in the middle of the street, Kelly has partners from nowhere: two passing sailors, two girls, then two more girls, all fitted out in various bright colour combinations and all knowing exactly the steps they need to know, a whole small chorus line. This is not putting on a show, this is magically converting a real town and its denizens into a show. The scene ends when Kelly leaps on to the side of his open-top MG, slides down into his seat, and drives off, the music chasing him. If Astaire suggests elegance and risk, Kelly offers us the perfect and unlikely combination of grace and energy. I used to think he was working a bit too hard at his routines – this is part of what is implied when people call him athletic – but that was a long time ago, and I don't know how I could have got such a wrong-headed idea. Watch him curtail one of his fast glides on his roller-skates in *It's Always Fair Weather* (1955). He stops dead on the mark, as if he had never been moving at all. It's a sort of miracle, and there is not the slightest sense of strain; just an ordinary guy doing extraordinary things.

The American musical has had some striking successes since the 1950s, but the real home of the genre is now on another continent. Since the 1970s, the Indian film industry generally has outgrown its American counterpart by some distance. Of course, not all of its films are musicals, far from it; but the musical is hugely popular in India, and many films that in other cultures would be about as far from music as anything could be turn effectively to song or dance at some point. Mani Rathnam's *Bombay* (1995), for example, which has been compared to Spielberg's *Schindler's List* (1993), is an eloquent case. While the very idea of singing in the Spielberg movie would seem to shift it into the territory of Mel Brooks, nothing of the kind happens in the Indian film, a melancholy romance forms a memorable response to a historical nightmare.

Visually, Indian musicals owe a great deal to Hollywood, and often look as if they borrowed their colours from MGM and their high-angle camera shots from Busby Berkeley. But of course, they have a very long indigenous tradition of dance and myth behind them, and the combinations of East and West on the screen are often remarkable, leave you shaking your head at the elegant, rapid crossovers, the 'modern' movement of this ancient dance form, the 'ancient' accent of this thoroughly modern chorus. The numbers are often very long, and usually have a narrative thread of attraction and resistance between boy and girl. The girl is usually in control, often scornful; the boy a little bewildered, but of course he is the prize, he doesn't have to be smart. There has been a reciprocal influence, and Baz Luhrmann has acknowledged the influence of the Indian industry on his own brightly coloured musical *Moulin Rouge* (2001).

So what about the stretch across the genre? Does it undo the genre as such? It undoes easy generalizations, and there are no thematic preoccupations that will carry across musicals as they will across westerns. But the twinning of music and ordinary life, or the simulation of ordinary life, beautifully represented by the song and dance number at the end of *Slumdog Millionaire* (2008), not in itself a musical, is surely a metaphor or a promise of considerable power. The bright colours and the noise become decor and disco. The railway station, once the location of panic and poverty and violence, becomes scenery. The beat is heavy and fast, the hero and heroine line up together, happily stomping in the front row of a vast dancing crowd. Even the trains look as if they want to get in on the act.

Whether the figure who shifts from talking to singing or from walking to dancing is Astaire or Kelly or Doris Day or Catherine Deneuve or Freida Pinto, a sense of life's lyrical capacities is asserted. The great musicals, we might say, are the ones where such singing and dancing feel, if not natural, at least vividly called for; and the lesser works are the ones where the music just interrupts the action, or the action plods along until the music returns.

Gangster films, which for the purpose of the present discussion I'm separating from the much larger category of crime films (murder mysteries, thrillers, caper movies, police procedurals, and many more), are a far more concentrated affair than musicals, even than westerns, and their mythology, although complex and shifting, is comparatively easy to describe. A good instance, although not a great movie, is Michael Mann's recent *Public Enemies* (2009), starring Johnny Depp as the gloomy, charismatic Dillinger. This film is all romance, Depp is the lonely free spirit tracked by an ugly legal system and betrayed by his friends. Crime is freedom, and if we have any moral reservations at all about Depp's choice of career, they are swept away by the scene in which he walks into a police station, passes the time of day with a couple of cops who don't recognize him, dips into a filing cabinet, looks at the large file they have on him, and walks out. After such style, what complaints are possible?

This glamorizing of the gangster was there from the genre's origin, and can't ever be fully separated from it. But of course, it can be questioned, and is. The queries are rather half-hearted in early classics like *Scarface* (1932) and *The Public Enemy* (1931), where we learn that rats do better than humans in the rat race, and crime doesn't pay – or at least, doesn't pay very well in the currency of comfort and the long life. It can't be all bad to go out in a self-orchestrated apotheosis, as Edward G. Robinson does in *Little Caesar* (1931), crying 'Mother of Mercy, is this the end of Rico?' – or in a blast of light, as James Cagney does in *White Heat* (1949), exploding into nothingness after repeating the phrase his (now dead) mother always used as career encouragement, 'Top of the world, Ma'.

'The real city', Robert Warshow shrewdly wrote, 'produces only criminals; the imaginary city produces the gangster: he is what we want to be and what we are afraid we may become'. Warshow goes on to make an extraordinary suggestion, which shows how thoroughly he himself has romanticized America rather than the gangster, whom he deems to express 'that part of the psyche which rejects the qualities and demands of modern life, which rejects "Americanism" itself'. Can this be? Surely the gangster is modern life, he is Americanism personified? He is now, and has been since the 1970s, and Pauline Kael made the same point against Warshow in her review of *The Godfather* (1972). This is in part because the gangster has become smoother, his operations more clandestine and corporate, but in even larger part, we are witnessing a shift in the very terms of Warshow's judgement. 'Modern life' and 'Americanism', we realize with more than a slight shock, once suggested, at least to some people, a progressive, liberal civil society and the rule of law; as distinct from venture capital and the inalienable right to make money on and off the edges of legality.

This is precisely the moral and social scene of Coppola's *Godfather* movies, and especially the second (1974), in which crime pays abundantly but produces a bleak isolation among the beneficiaries, precisely because there is nothing they can't do.

When Michael Corleone's chief adviser asks him why he feels he has to kill everyone, Michael replies with weary righteousness, as if the thing were too obvious to need saying: 'I don't feel I have to kill everybody, Tom. Just my enemies.' At one moment late in this film, Michael and his men are planning to dispose of a heavily guarded gangster, already in custody. Someone says they can't do it, it would be like trying to kill the President (a possibility not unheard of in American movies or American history). Michael says with gloomy, precise emphasis, stretching out the first two clauses, 'If anything in this life is certain, if history has taught us anything, it's that you can kill anybody.'

One of the greatest films of the genre, Scorsese's *Goodfellas* (1990), is also perhaps the funniest thoroughly frightening movie ever made. Here's how it starts. We see a large American car from the back, driving at night on the wrong, that is, on the left side of the road. The car swerves into the right lane, the camera stays in the left, catches up, comes alongside the car. The screen goes dark and a title says, 'New York, 1970'. There are three men in the car, one of them (Ray Liotta) noticeably younger than the other two (Robert de Niro, Joe Pesci). The young man is driving, and thinks he hears a noise coming from the car's boot. Inspection reveals a man wrapped in a bloodstained sheet and, alas, still alive: unfinished business. Pesci drives his knife into the man six or seven times. De Niro shoots the man four times. Liotta steps forward to close the boot, and we hear his voice on the soundtrack saying, 'As far back as I can remember I always wanted to be a gangster.' He slams the boot shut, the frame freezes on his slightly startled face, and the music begins, a hefty big band sound. Just before the title of the film flashes across the screen, the vocalist makes his entry. It's Tony Bennett singing 'From Rags to Riches'.

It's the American dream, but of course, Liotta is saying far more than he can understand. He always wanted to be a gangster, but was this what being a gangster meant? This worry is still chasing him late in the movie, in what Scorsese says is one of his favourite sequences from his own works. At this point, Liotta is multi-tasking, fully in the grip of the delusion that he is in control of everything. He picks his brother up from the hospital, parks an assignment of guns in his mother-in-law's garage, makes a drug delivery, and cooks dinner at home, dropping by from time to time to check on the cutlets and the sauce. All the while, he is being pursued by a narcotics agency helicopter; narrating the whole story in voice-over; snorting cocaine, constantly sweating, manifestly manic, on the verge of breakdown, but still crazily congratulating himself on getting so many things done at once. When he is finally arrested in his car, he says, 'For a second I thought I was dead. Then when I heard all the noise I knew they were cops.' He always wanted to be a gangster, and doesn't have much of an option any more. But what he really has wanted is to be the person in charge, a figure whose speed and efficiency he can himself admire. He is like one of those characters in Joseph Conrad who wonder at their own courage because they don't feel afraid – they're so scared that their minds don't have any space for how they feel. We're not laughing, but the structure of desperation here is deeply comic.

Scorsese stays (just) within the parameters of the genre film but gives us a full, hectic blast of the American fantasy of power and success in a pathological mode. And he has taken away one of the staple comforts of the genre, an essential aspect of *The Godfather* movies, for instance: the thought of *organized* crime, as if organization were always better than disorder, and the world of professional crime had never heard of accidents. Gangster movies are about, among many other things, the banishment of the merely random, death without a reason: violence controlled and properly distributed.

The gangster film is the most American of genres not because there are no gangsters anywhere else, but because no other culture thrives so on the romance of capital, the declension that turns money into power and power into freedom. Even so, there have been memorable contributions to the tradition from elsewhere. There are, for example: Sergio Leone's *Once Upon a Time in America* (1984), too grand and gloomy for the term 'spaghetti gangster' even to cross our minds; Mike Hodges' *Get Carter* (1971) and John Mackenzie's *The Long Good Friday* (1980); a series of stylish French films by Jean-Pierre Melville, especially *Le Samourai* (1967); and a host of fine Hong Kong movies, notably *Infernal Affairs* (2002), on which Scorsese based his film *The Departed* (2006).

There are also some interesting asides and epilogues. Fans of the genre were outraged recently when Wilder's antic comedy *Some Like It Hot* (1959) was listed on a website as a gangster movie, and we can understand their concern. But it is part of the authority of the form that an accidental encounter with the St Valentine's Day Massacre could become a plot device; and the gangsters in the film are only a small parodic step away, and sometimes not even that, from their 'serious' counterparts. I think too of the ageing gunmen in Jim Jarmusch's *Ghost Dog* (1999). They run up the stairs like trained killers, but they stand panting like old men outside their victim's door. Surely this can't be part of the script? Where is the editor who takes care of ageing? As with all working genres, the gangster film engages with its limits. All these strutting or muttering men deal in death and often end in terrible disaster – this way, they are saved from time and ordinariness, from the comedy that would make them resemble the rest of us.

The old friend. This set of films can't quite be a genre because there are no rules for its construction, and you can't create a member of the group intentionally. You can make good or bad westerns or musicals or gangster films, and the genre won't be in doubt. But you can't make a movie people will be certain to cherish, any more than you can make your companions love you if their attentions are elsewhere. Nevertheless, this near-genre tells us a lot about the medium and about genre itself; we remember those nebulous old stories not just because they are in the air and get repeated, but because we are fond of them, they are part of who we are when we think about who we are. This note of affection is important: we are not contending that these films are great, only that we can't do without them.

Here are some features of movies as old friends. We are never bored by any of them – or if we are bored, it is in a comfortable, nostalgic fashion. We never say not again, only welcome back. We like to think they have scarcely been away. They are full of remarks and gimmicks we never tire of imitating or describing. We say, 'Play it again, Sam' (or 'Play it, Sam', if we're feeling pedantic); we say 'Walk this way'; we can't get enough of Paul Henreid lighting two cigarettes at once in *Now Voyager* (1942); we lip-synch half the lines in *The Rocky Horror Picture Show* (1975); cry once again when Tootie beheads her snowmen in *Meet Me in St Louis* (1944). Every actor in these movies is perfectly what he or she is supposed to be, neither more nor less. The stiff upper lip of C. Aubrey Smith as Colonel Sapt in *The Prisoner of Zenda* (1937) set the gold standard for stiff upper lips; no dog on film was ever more on cue or tuned into dialogue than Toto – of course, he knows they're not in Kansas any more. And if a bad joke is repeated once – the neighing horses in *Young Frankenstein* (1974), say, every time Frau Blücher is mentioned – it is repeated *ad nauseam*, or as far as what would be nausea if we didn't love the movie so much.

Of course, we share some of these memories, or many of us do. I couldn't even talk of a near-genre if we didn't, and I hope the above evocations don't add up to a merely private listing. But the sharing of particular memories is not essential, as it would be in the case of a real genre. What's essential is the *kind* of memory that is shared, the zone of affection, the mark of a relation to a popular medium. Surely most moviegoers, as distinct from cinephiles, have some such feeling about what they have seen, about a whole realm of what they have seen. It's interesting too that we can often feel this way about old TV programmes as well as films, so my earlier notion of footage returns here: moving pictures placed before us, and then placed before us again.

What such lingering, sentimental affections suggest is how much any genre needs our care. If we can't make a genre out of the old friend, we can come very close; close enough to remind ourselves that genre itself depends so thoroughly on our fondness and tolerance for its repetitive ways. It can use all the conventions it wants to, all the conventions it has ever heard of, but it will only come alive if those conventions are alive for us, and in this sense, even the genres that terrify us are our good friends, otherwise they wouldn't be genres. If 'stars matter', as Dyer says, 'because they act out aspects of life that matter to us', then genres are the climates in which stars live, modes of imaginatively recycling our worries – about the law, about our chances of happiness, about our dreams of immunity from guilt or punishment, about much else. And perhaps these are not just worries. As Fredric Jameson suggests, we may actually, in the midst of our pleasure, be working through our less acceptable suspicions, slipping 'our political thoughts past a liberal and anti-political censorship'.

Deaths of the cinema

Quentin Tarantino's *Inglourious Basterds* (2009) ends with a spectacular fire that would have been hyperbolic and full of self-reference even if the film had been made much earlier. You can hardly burn a cinema on screen without making some sort of comment on the art. In the early 21st century, though, such a sequence can only look like a desperate memorial to a whole habit and culture. During the Second World War, a French-Jewish cinema-owner, who has already escaped from the occupying Nazis once, decides to set fire to her own building, and herself with it, emblematically using her nitrate stock as chief combustible. The movie-house is showing a German war movie, but that's not her main reason. It's a gala premiere, and several of the Reich's grandees are to be there: Hitler, Goebbels, Goering, Bormann. They all go up in flames, a very satisfying counterfactual catch.

We may think of the famous line uttered by the devil in Bulgakov's *The Master and Margarita*: 'manuscripts don't burn'. They don't if the devil takes an interest in them. Otherwise they burn beautifully, as Bulgakov himself well knew. Film burns, cinemas burn, the good guys and the bad guys burn. One of the things Tarantino is suggesting, surely, is that if the art of film is ending, it should perform its departure in a spectacular way, should rage against the dying of the work of light. And it should go out in a good cause – that is, a good filmic cause, like killing film Nazis. There's nothing to done about the actual Nazis, who died in different ways and times, but Tarantino's Germans will obligingly provide a target every time the film is remembered. Even burned films and manuscripts may have afterlives, and that is part of what Bulgakov's devil is saying.

The death of cinema has been announced many times, starting as long ago as the 1920s and the arrival of sound. But there has been a real flurry of such claims in the last ten or fifteen years, and for all kinds of reasons. Death is an extreme proposition in any context, and in other instances, like the famous death of God and the ever-recurring deaths of the author and the novel, the proclamation seems to have led to nothing but revival after revival. Still, something is happening to provoke these assertions and arguments, and it's worth trying to find out what it is – especially if it turns out to be several different things.

For the old guard of the French magazine *Cahiers du cinéma*, the death of the cinema, which they dated to the 1990s, meant what looked like the permanent absence of films they could admire, that curious mixture of commerce and art that they had welcomed since the 1950s, based neither more nor less on Bresson and Godard than on Hitchcock and Nicholas Ray. By the same token, it meant the unwelcome life of the films they didn't like, a version of the old cinema of quality resurgent and triumphant: Téchiné's *Scene of the Crime* (1986), Blier's *Merci la vie* (1991), Carax's *The Lovers on the Bridge* (1991). Finally, the *Cahiers* themselves went over to this new/old market, and became a glossy branch of its advertising.

Susan Sontag's sense of the cinema's death is similar:

> It's not that you can't look forward anymore to new films that you can admire. But such films not only have to be exceptions – that's true of great achievements in any art. They have to be actual violations of the norms and practices that now govern movie making everywhere in the capitalist and would-be capitalist world.

For others, the death was not about film content or style but about technology, and specifically the possibility of seeing films at home – the very possibility flirted with and abandoned in the earliest days of cinema, and now presenting itself, for some, as a kind of doom. Hadn't television already taken care of this question in the 1950s? Not quite. It had provided serious commercial competition and it had eaten into audiences, driven film studios into attempts to do things with the large screens and special effects only cinemas could properly display. This game is still going on, with I-Max, the revival of 3-D vision, and several related devices. When I recently walked into a cinema and encountered a whole tiered room full of faces equipped with white-edged plastic glasses, the sight was more startling than anything in the film I had come to see, not least because I thought I had fallen back into the 1950s. But the small screen itself didn't alter the world so much as long as it belonged to a television set, and not to a video recorder-player. There were scheduled programmes on television and in the cinema; no one was interfering with film time.

The new arrangements, born with the invention of Betamax and VHS machines, brought three radical changes, often mistaken for one. Only two of them are of immediate importance for film. The director Peter Greenaway, for example, dramatically asserted that the remote control apparatus had destroyed film, but this is only a tiny piece of the tale. We could always pause, stop, or rewind a film at home without a remote control device. Still, this choice of pacing was the first change that mattered: we could take a break, and watch the same scene as many times as we liked; we could skip whole sequences without having to close our eyes or leave the room. The second change, more significant for television than for film, had to do with recording, and meant that we no longer needed to watch shows when they were screened, so that, theoretically, the whole notion of programming had gone out of the window. And the third change was that we could watch films at home, we could buy them or rent them, and would never have to set foot or posterior in a cinema again if we didn't want to.

The effects I've just described are often associated with digital technology, and this too easy association represents a slight historical slippage. Nothing digital about VHS, and it's important to see which technology is doing what. But as VHS vanishes, and laser-discs enter the museums of our recent history, it will be a digital technology that delivers these same results to us, so the association will become true even if it wasn't true to start with.

However, 'digital' means many other things as well: new forms of photography and sound recording, new forms of image transfer, new modes of collaboration between different data systems, and so on. Digital photography is now standard for film documentaries, and many feature films are shot digitally and then transferred to analogue form for projection. Many films *look* as if they have been digitally composed, whatever cameras have been used, because the imagined space on screen has been put together after the photographed fact – so that we see St Paul's and Big Ben, for example, close together in the same shot (in *The Mummy Returns*, 2001) and a whole re-imagined London geography in Guy Ritchie's *Sherlock Holmes* (2009). Even those of us who don't have a great eye for visual differences can distinguish between a film space composed *for* the camera (Cavell: a film is always a film of something), where people and objects were arranged in (some sort of) reality before they were photographed, and a film space composed *in* a camera, so that nothing needs to have been literally where it was before the camera got to work.

And of course, for those who have a real eye there is all the difference in the world between any form of reproduction of a film, digital or not, and the same film run through an actual projector at the right speed. It seems appropriate to speak of a death here, since something that was once to be seen – Peter Bogdanovich recalls being able to see the shimmer of silver on old silver nitrate films – is just not to be seen any more. I'm less sure that being able to stop the film and see it at home – if this can be abstracted from the visual quality of what's seen – has to represent a loss as well as a change. But of course, if your idea of cinema includes everything that preceded the change – going to a movie-house, paying for your ticket, sitting in the dark for a specific of period of time watching a film that could not pause or run backwards – the change will only feel like loss.

But now consider these not at all exceptional facts and possibilities. Film is still big business, or can be. The highest grossing Indian films have made between 200 and 350 million dollars each. For the US, the comparable figures are between 500 and 750 million. Most films we see on a big screen continue to be films in the old sense, however they began life. Conversely, films are cheaper to make than ever, and more films are being made than ever before. Some time in the course of today, no doubt, one member or another of your family (or mine) will film some moving images, and email them to friends or place them on Facebook. This will be a (piece of) film, but it won't be on film. I have many films on my bookshelves, and quite a few books on a handheld device. The best way to see Dreyer's *The Passion of Joan of Arc* is via a 35-mm projector, but the complete film I get for free on an I-phone, courtesy of YouTube, has better definition than any version I can see through a television screen or on a full-size

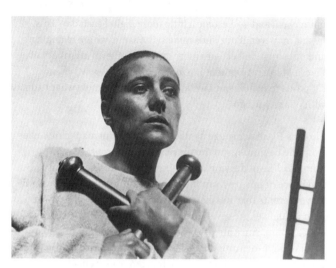

10. Silence speaks

computer. Anyone more plugged in to current technology could multiply these criss-crossing stories in all kinds of ways.

The new media allow us better access at least to the content of the old media than we have ever had. Tag Gallagher is on record as saying that 'for a movie lover there's been no better time to be alive – with all due respect for those who claim that only nitrate is worth watching'. 'It starts to become possible', Jonathan Rosenbaum writes, 'to conceive of a new kind of cinephilia', a love of films which doesn't depend on the old experience of cinema. Marshall McLuhan was wrong: the medium is not the message. The medium is the medium, and storage and delivery are storage and delivery. We don't have to get hung up on old modes of memory and transport, and we don't have to assume the newest are always the best.

But then again, Marshall McLuhan was also right: no medium, once we have started living with it, leaves our habits of perception untouched, and we become a little more digital each day. This means that even if our films remain the same, we are changing, and our situation becomes more and more like an aftermath of that of Margaret Dumont in *Duck Soup*: we know we are not supposed to believe our own eyes, but we don't know what to do with our scepticism.

Thomas Elsaesser suggests that successive cinema technologies from the beginnings to the present day may represent a 'complex line of development where each marks a step in the severance of images from their material referents'. These are the very referents that Barthes said that photography always carried with it, and yet the severance actually looks like a closer and closer union, since almost every new breakthrough in visual media – high-definition television, motion capture on film, for example – is said to increase the image's reality effect, and it does. But only the effect. The riddle assumes its perfect, elegant shape. The less unaltered reality there is in the image, in the form of a trace or print or shadow, the more what we see looks like reality – to the point where nothing can look authentic on a screen without vast amounts of artifice going into its transmission. What Bazin called our 'obsession with realism' can be allayed or tempered only by more and more sophisticated forms of fabrication. This riddle was always part of film technology to some degree, and it was what Walter Benjamin was glancing at when he wrote of the blue flower in the land of technology, the apparently unassisted natural beauty that requires more assistance than the wildest sort of fantasy. In this perspective, special effects at their best don't look special, because they don't look like effects. But even Benjamin didn't imagine the flower would just keep getting bluer, and the endlessness of the riddle and its permanent spiralling contradictions have fully dawned on us only lately.

Steve Edwards asks 'to what extent are digital images photographs?', and answers that both digital and chemical photography represent a presumably pre-existent world. 'But, as pixels are progressively transformed, this relation is weakened.'

The relation of picture to world was always weaker than the grand myths of photography claimed, and 'digital' is in one sense just a name for our belated sense of how much manipulation is possible in any mode of imagery. Still, as Edwards points out, if a picture of a car is transformed on a computer into a picture of a bike, we have to wonder whether we should still call the result a photograph. It's a wonderful question, and I think the answer is that unless we knew the story of the transformation, we would call it a photograph – of a bike.

To believe that a digital film cannot picture the world as it is just because the computer *could* alter the image is in its way as drastic an option as any naïve faith in the old photography, with its dream of natural origins and honest technology, its assumption that 0s and 1s can't possibly create any sort of semblance of reality, that only analogue procedures are to be trusted. To understand that both digital and analogue formats can be radically rearranged, and to grasp how much digital technology has raised the stakes in such a game, is to return to the place where we perhaps always were. We decide on the truthfulness of film, or its copying or conjuring of reality, as we decide on all other questions of truth and reality: by collecting evidence, making comparisons, believing our own eyes, and working out what else to believe as well.

What is broken or dead or dispersed in the digital age is the complex of meanings once defined by film: art, industry, exhibition space, habit, celebrity orbit. Even the Multiplex will probably fade away, once films start to be downloaded there from a server rather than shipped to individual locations; and DVDs may well follow the already promised path of CDs. We shall watch films by ordering them up from an equivalent of I-Tunes – as many people already do. I'm sure all kinds of further wreckages of our customs are in store.

But I believe that two senses of film will remain, one quite strict, the other very loose – and it's the pull between them, I suggest, that will help to preserve the term's life. Could the name change? Might we come to call 'film' in either or both of these senses something else? We might; but I'm guessing we won't.

The two senses are these. A film is a story or a proposition (remember the dictionary's cautious recital: 'a cinematographic representation of a story, drama, episode, event, etc.') that is shaped, angled, finite, intended, whether it is a documentary, an art installation, a bit of gritty realism, or a full-blown fantasy. When people say they have been watching a film, this is what we take them to mean. A film-maker is a person who makes such things. The other sense is also one I evoked much earlier, that of footage: fragments or sequences, short or long, fictive or actual, of motion caught in the act. These pieces may add up to a film in the first sense, but it's part of the freedom of the form that they don't have to, and their value will often lie in their accidental feel, even if it's faked.

In this respect, digital film retains part of an old loyalty to photography. Early cinema is full of stories about embarrassing moments caught on film by accident, and, in Tom Gunning's words, 'the sense of the camera as the nonhuman agent of truth is emphasized by the fact that the filming is often accidental'. The camera might lie, we could say, but accidents can't. Noel Burch's argument is important here: that film is peculiarly subject to chance and yet has made its history by seeking to overcome it: 'the world of sheer chance...is usually banished by most film-makers to some forgotten corner of off-screen space'. Film in my first sense seeks to defeat film in the second sense. We might feel that the very greatest films, like Visconti's *The Leopard* (1963), succeed but only just; or, like Buñuel's *Los Olvidados* (1950), fail but not by much.

It looks as if we may care about film because it responds so perfectly to what Leo Charney and Vanessa Schwartz identify as our 'impulse to define, fix, and represent isolated moments in the face of modernity's distractions and sensations', but it does that only when we treat it, as we often do, as a form of rolling photography. Film in its magical, animating mode doesn't define, fix, or even represent anything, doesn't capture, hold, or freeze, it lets its objects run, lends them the life we thought they had lost; and shaped or ragged, it mixes what we remember with what we dream and offers us an image of movement that we often can't quite believe and almost never can deny. Just watch those children on your mobile phone. Or Marlene Dietrich lifting her ironic eyebrow one more time.

References

Chapter 1

Mary Ann Doane, *The Emergence of Cinematic Time* (Cambridge and London: Harvard University Press, 2002), p. 172.

Sandra Aamodt and Sam Wang, *Welcome to Your Brain* (New York, Berlin, London: Bloomsbury, 2008), p. 47.

Joseph and Barbara Anderson, 'The Myth of Persistence of Vision Revisited', *Journal of Film and Video*, 45(1) (Spring 1993).

Hollis Frampton, 'Lecture', in P. Adams Sitney (ed.), *The Avant-Garde Film* (New York: New York University Press, 1978), p. 279.

Virginia Woolf, 'The Cinema', in *The Captain's Death-Bed and Other Essays* (New York and London: Harcourt Brace Jovanovich, 1978), p. 181.

Walter Benjamin, 'A Small History of Photography', in *One Way Street and Other Writings*, tr. Edmund Jephcott and Kingsley Shorter (London: Verso Books, 1979), pp. 242–3.

Roland Barthes, *Camera Lucida*, tr. Richard Howard (New York: Hill and Wang, 1981), pp. 28, 5, 79, 90, 96.

André Bazin, *What is Cinema?* Volume 1, tr. Hugh Gray (Berkeley: University of California Press, 1967), pp. 12, 29, 30.

Aristotle, *Poetics*, tr. S. H. Butcher (New York: Hill and Wang, 1961), pp. 55, 56.

Patricia Aufderheide, *Documentary Film: A Very Short Introduction* (Oxford, New York: Oxford University Press, 2007), p. 56.

Wheeler Winston Dixon and Gwendolyn Audrey Foster, *A Short History of Film* (New Brunswick: Rutgers University Press, 2008), pp. 1–3.

Charles Musser, 'Introducing Cinema to the American Public', in Gregory A. Waller (ed.), *Moviegoing in America* (Oxford and Malden, Mass.: Blackwell, 2002), p. 13.

Noel Burch, *Theory of Film Practice*, tr. Helen R. Lane (Princeton: Princeton University Press, 1981), p. 12.

Luis Buñuel, 'Dreyer's *Joan of Arc*', in Francisco Aranda (ed.), *Luis Buñuel* (New York: Da Capo, 1978), p. 268.

P. Adams Sitney, *Modernist Montage* (New York: Columbia University Press, 1990), p. 17.

Lev Kuleshov, *Kuleshov on Film*, tr. Ron Levaco (Berkeley, Los Angeles, London: University of California Press, 1974), p. 48.

Sean Cubitt, *The Cinema Effect* (Cambridge, Mass.: MIT Press, 2004), p. 97.

Donald Crafton, *Before Mickey* (Chicago: University of Chicago Press, 1993), pp. 8, 12, 52.

Chapter 2

Lillian Ross, 'With Fellini', *The New Yorker*, 24 June 1985.

John Gregory Dunne, *Monster* (New York: Random House, 1997).

André Bazin, *What is Cinema?* Volume 1, tr. Hugh Gray (Berkeley: University of California Press, 1967), pp. 74, 83, 9, xviii.

Peter Biskind, *Star: How Warren Beatty Seduced America* (New York: Simon & Schuster, 2011), p. 160.

Richard Dyer, *Heavenly Bodies: Film Stars and Society* (London: Routledge, 2003), p. 17.

Laura Mulvey, *Death 24x a Second* (London: Reaktion Books, 2006), pp. 17, 67, 69.

Robert Desnos, *Cinéma* (Paris: Gallimard, 1966), p. 9.

Alain Badiou, 'Du cinéma comme emblème démocratique', *Critique*, January–February 2005, p. 9.

Roland Barthes, *Mythologies*, tr. Annette Lavers (New York: Hill and Wang, 1972), pp. 27–8.

Buñuel's phrase is 'the pititful geography of their faces'. Quoted in Francisco Aranda, *Luis Buñuel: A Critical Biography*, tr. and ed. David Robinson (New York: Da Capo, 1976), p. 268.

Luis Buñuel, *Mon dernier soupir* (Paris: Robert Laffont, 1982), p. 173.

William Rothman, *Documentary Film Classics* (Cambridge: Cambridge University Press, 1997), pp. 27, 24, 112, 44.

Jacques Rancière, *La fable cinématographique* (Paris: Seuil, 2001), pp. 201–2.

Philip Lopate, *Notes on Night and Fog* (New York: Criterion Collection, 2003).

Emilie Bickerton, *A Short History of Cahiers du Cinema* (London: Verso, 2009), p. 2.

Theodor W. Adorno, *Minima Moralia*, tr. E. F. N. Jephcott (London: Verso, 1978), p. 163.

Jean-Luc Godard, *Histoire(s) du cinéma* (Paris: Gallimard, 1998), p. 86.

Stuart Galbraith IV, *The Emperor and the Wolf* (London and New York: Faber and Faber, 2001), p. 253.

A. L. Rees, *A History of Experimental Film and Video* (London: BFI Publishing, 1999), p. viii.

Leo Charney and Vanessa Schwartz (eds.), *Cinema and the Invention of Modern Life* (Berkeley, Los Angeles, London: University of California Press, 1995), p. 6.

Hollis Frampton, 'A Pentagram for Conjuring the Narrative', in P. Adams Sitney (ed.), *The Avant-Garde Film* (New York: New York University Press, 1978), p. 284.

François Truffaut, 'Une certain tendance du cinéma français', *Cahiers du cinéma*, January 1954.

François Truffaut, 'Ali Baba et la politique des auteurs', *Cahiers du cinéma*, February 1955.

Andrew Sarris, *The American Cinema* (New York: Da Capo, 1996), pp. 29–30.

David Lynch, *Catching the Big Fish* (New York: Tarcher, 2007), p. 51.

Esther Leslie, *Hollywood Flatlands* (London: Verso, 2002), pp. 289, 291.

Stanley Cavell, *The World Viewed* (Cambridge, Mass.: Harvard University Press 1979), pp. 168, 170, 171.

William Paul, 'The K-Mart Audience at the Mall Movies', in Gregory A. Waller (ed.), *Moviegoing in America* (Oxford and Malden, Mass.: Blackwell, 2002), p. 286.

Stephen Barber, *Abandoned Images: Film and Film's End* (London: Reaktion Books, 2010), pp. 12, 7, 26, 88, 8.

John Eberson, 'A Description of the Capitol Theater, Chicago (1925)', in Gregory A. Waller (ed.), *Moviegoing in America* (Oxford and Malden, Mass.: Blackwell, 2002), p. 107.

Jacques Rancière, 'L'affect indécis', *Critique*, January–February 2005, p. 154.

Philip Larkin, 'Poetry of Departures', in *The Less Deceived* (London: Faber, 1955), p. 22.

George N. Fenin and William K. Everson, *The Western: From Silents to the Seventies* (New York: Penguin, 1977), *passim*.

Robert Warshow, *The Immediate Experience* (Cambridge, Mass.: Harvard University Press, 2002), pp. 100, 107.

Fredric Jameson, *The Geopolitical Aesthetic: Cinema and Space in the World System* (Bloomington and London: Indiana University Press/BFI Publishing, 1992), p. 9.

Jonathan Rosenbaum, *Goodbye Cinema, Hello Cinephilia* (Chicago: University of Chicago Press, 2010), pp. xii, 5.

Thomas Elsaesser, 'Early Film History and Multimedia', in Wendy Chun and Tom Keenan (eds.), *New Media, Old Media* (New York: Routledge, 2006), p. 23.

Steve Edwards, *Photography: A Very Short Introduction* (Oxford: Oxford University Press, 2006), p. 132.

Tom Gunning, 'Tracing the Individual Body', in Leo Charney and Vanessa Schwartz (eds.), *Cinema and the Invention of Modern Life* (Berkeley and London: University of California Press, 1995), p. 36.

Noël Burch, *Theory of Film Practice* (Princeton: Princeton University Pres, 1981), p. 118.

Charney and Schwartz (eds.), 'Introduction', *Cinema and the Invention of Modern Life*, p. 3.

Further reading

Lawrence Alloway, *Violent America: The Movies, 1946–1964* (New York: Museum of Modern Art, 1971).

Rick Altman, *The American Film Musical* (Bloomington, Indiana: Indiana University Press, 1987).

Dudley Andrew, *What Cinema Is* (Oxford: Blackwell, 2010).

Rudolf Arnheim, *Film as Art* (London: Faber, 1958).

Patricia Aufderheide, *Documentary Film: A Very Short Introduction* (Oxford and New York: Oxford University Press, 2007).

Antoine de Baecque, *La Cinéphilie* (Paris: Fayard, 2003).

Béla Balázs, *Theory of the Film*, tr. Edith Bone (New York: Dover, 1970).

Tino Balio, *The American Film Industry* (Madison: University of Wisconsin Press, 1976).

Tino Balio, *Grand Design* (New York: Scribner, 1993).

Stephen Barber, *Abandoned Images: Film and Film's End* (London: Reaktion Books, 2010).

Roland Barthes, *Camera Lucida*, tr. Richard Howard (New York: Hill and Wang, 1981).

Roland Barthes, *Mythologies*, tr. Annette Lavers (New York: Hill and Wang, 1972).

André Bazin, *What is Cinema?*, tr. Hugh Gray (Berkeley, Los Angeles, and London: University of California Press, 1967).

Walter Benjamin, *One Way Street and Other Writings*, tr. Edmund Jephcott and Kingsley Shorter (London: Verso Books, 1979).

Walter Benjamin, *Selected Writings*, Volume 4, tr. Edmund Jephcott and others (Cambridge, Mass.: Harvard University Press, 2003).

Emilie Bickerton, *A Short History of Cahiers du Cinéma* (London and
New York: Verso, 2009).

D. Bordwell, *Ozu and the Poetics of Cinema* (Princeton: Princeton
University Press, 1988).

D. Bordwell, *On the History of Film Style* (Cambridge, Mass.: Harvard
University Press, 1997).

D. Bordwell, *Planet Hong Kong* (Cambridge, Mass.: Harvard
University Press, 2000).

Steven T. Brown, *Cinema Anime* (London: Palgrave Macmillan,
2006).

K. Brownlow, *The Parade's Gone By* (New York: Knopf, 1968).

Noel Burch, *Theory of Film Practice*, tr. Helen R. Lane (Princeton:
Princeton University Press, 1981).

Noel Burch, *To the Distant Observer*, ed. Annette Michelson (Berkeley,
Los Angeles, and London: University of California Press, 1979).

Noel Burch, *Life to Those Shadows*, tr. and ed. Ben Brewster (Berkeley,
Los Angeles, and London: University of California Press, 1990).

Stanley Cavell, *The World Viewed* (Cambridge, Mass.: Harvard
University Press, 1971).

Stanley Cavell, *Pursuits of Happiness* (Cambridge, Mass.: Harvard
University Press, 1981).

Leo Charney and Vanessa Schwartz (eds.), *Cinema and the Invention
of Modern Life* (Berkeley, Los Angeles, and London: University of
California Press, 1995).

Wendy Chun and Thomas Keenan (eds.), *New Media, Old Media* (New
York and London: Routledge, 2006).

David A. Cook, *A History of Narrative Film* (New York: Norton,
2004).

Donald Crafton, *Before Mickey* (Chicago: University of Chicago Press,
1993).

Donald Crafton, *The Talkies* (Berkeley, Los Angeles, and London:
University of California Press, 1997).

Jonathan Crary, *Techniques of the Observer* (Cambridge, Mass.: MIT
Press, 1990).

Sean Cubitt, *The Cinema Effect* (Cambridge, Mass.: MIT Press, 2004).

Gilles Deleuze, *Cinéma 1 and 2* (Paris: Minuit, 1986, 1989).

Robert Desnos, *Cinéma* (Paris: Gallimard, 1966).

Wheeler Winston Dixon and Gwendolyn Audrey Foster, *A Short
History of Film* (New Brunswick: Rutgers University Press,
2008).

Mary Anne Doane, *The Emergence of Cinematic Time* (Cambridge, Mass. and London: Harvard University Press, 2002).

John Gregory Dunne, *Studio* (New York: Farrar, Straus and Giroux, 1969).

John Gregory Dunne, *Monster* (New York: Random House, 1997).

Richard Dyer, *Heavenly Bodies: Film Stars and Society* (London: Routledge, 2003).

Steve Edwards, *Photography: A Very Short Introduction* (Oxford: Oxford University Press, 2006).

Sergei Eisenstein, *Film Form*, ed. and tr. Jan Leyda (New York: Harcourt Brace, 1949).

Lotte Eisner, *The Haunted Screen*, tr. Roger Greaves (Berkeley: University of California Press, 1969).

Thomas Elsaesser and Adam Barker (eds.), *Early Cinema* (London: BFI Publishing, 1990).

Christopher Finch, *The Art of Walt Disney: From Mickey Mouse to the Magic Kingdoms* (New York: H. N. Abrams, 1973).

Christine Gledhill and Linda Williams (eds.), *Reinventing Film Studies* (New York: Oxford University Press, 2000).

Jean-Luc Godard, *Histoires du cinéma* (Paris: Gallimard (book); Gaumont (DVD), both 1998).

Tom Gunning, *The Films of Fritz Lang* (London: BFI Publishing, 2000).

Mark Hansen, *New Philosophy for New Media* (Cambridge, Mass. and London: MIT Press, 2004).

Miriam Hansen, *Babel and Babylon* (Cambridge, Mass.: Harvard University Press, 1991).

Forsyth Hardy, *Grierson on Documentary* (Berkeley: University of California Press, 1966).

Dan Harries (ed.), *The New Media Book* (London: BFI Publishing, 2002).

Fredric Jameson, *The Geopolitical Aesthetic: Cinema and Space in the World System* (Bloomington and London: Indiana University Press/BFI Publishing, 1992).

Anton Kaes, *From Hitler to Heimat: The Return of History as Film* (Cambridge, Mass.: Harvard University Press, 1989).

Christian Keathley, *Cinephilia and History* (Bloomington: Indiana University Press, 2006).

Siegfried Kracauer, *From Caligari to Hitler* (Princeton: Princeton University Press, 1947).

Siegfried Kracauer, *Theory of Film* (New York: Oxford University Press, 1960).

Lev Kuleshov, *Kuleshov on Film*, tr. Ron Levaco (Berkeley, Los Angeles, and London: University of California Press, 1974).

Esther Leslie, *Hollywood Flatlands: Animation, Critical Theory and the Avant-Garde* (London and New York: Verso, 2002).

Richard Maltby, *Harmless Entertainment: Hollywood and the Ideology of Consensus* (Metuchen, NJ: Scarecrow Press, 1983).

Lev Manovich, *The Language of New Media* (Cambridge, Mass. and London: MIT Press, 2001).

Christian Metz, *Film Language*, tr. Michael Taylor (Chicago: University of Chicago Press, 1991).

James Monaco, *How to Read a Film* (New York: Oxford University Press, 2009).

Laura Mulvey, *Death 24x a Second* (London: Reaktion Books, 2006).

Laura Mulvey, *Visual and Other Pleasures* (New York: Palgrave Macmillan, 2009).

Charles Musser, *The Emergence of Cinema: The American Screen to 1907* (New York: Scribner, 1990).

Susan J. Napier, *Anime from Akira to Princess Mononoke* (New York: Palgrave, 2001).

Michael North, *Camera Works: Photography and the Twentieth-Century Word* (New York: Oxford University Press, 2005).

Geoffrey Nowell-Smith (ed.), *Oxford History of World Cinema* (Oxford and New York: Oxford University Press, 1997).

Geoffrey O'Brien, *Castaways of the Image Planet* (Washington, DC: Counterpoint, 2002).

S. S. Prawer, *Caligari's Children* (Oxford and New York: Oxford University Press, 1980).

V. I. Pudovkin, *Film Technique and Film Acting*, tr. and ed. Ivor Montagu (London: Vision, 1968).

Jacques Rancière, *La fable cinématographique* (Paris: Seuil, 2001).

Robert Ray, *A Certain Tendency of the Hollywood Cinema* (Princeton: Princeton University Press, 1985).

Robert Ray, *The ABCs of Classic Hollywood* (Oxford: Oxford University Press, 2008).

A. L. Rees, *A History of Experimental Film and Video* (London: BFI Publishing, 1999).

David Robinson, *From Peepshow to Palace* (New York: Columbia University Press, 1996).

D. N. Rodowick, *Gilles Deleuze's Time Machine* (Durham and London: Duke University Press, 1997).

Jonathan Rosenbaum, *Movie Wars* (Chicago: A. Cappella, 2000).

Jonathan Rosenbaum, *Goodbye Cinema, Hello Cinephilia* (Chicago: University of Chicago Press, 2010).

Paul Rotha, *The Film Till Now* (New York: Twayne, 1960).

William Rothman, *Documentary Film Classics* (Cambridge: Cambridge University Press, 1997).

Barry Salt, *Film Style and Technology* (London: Starword, 1983).

Andrew Sarris, *The American Cinema* (New York: Dutton, 1968).

Thomas Schatz, *Hollywood Genres* (Philadelphia: Temple University Press, 1981).

P. Adams Sitney (ed.), *The Avant-Garde Film* (New York: New York University Press, 1978).

P. Adams Sitney, *Modernist Montage* (New York: Columbia University Press, 1990).

Robert Sklar, *Movie-Made America* (New York: Random House, 1975).

Robert Sklar, *World History of Film* (New York: Harry N. Abrams, 2002).

Susan Sontag, *On Photography* (New York: Farrar, Straus and Giroux, 1977).

Garrett Stewart, *Between Film and Screen* (Chicago: University of Chicago Press, 1999).

Andrei Tarkovsky, *Sculpting in Time*, tr. Kitty Hunter-Blair (New York: Alfred A. Knopf, 1987).

Kristin Thompson, *Breaking the Glass Armor* (Princeton: Princeton University Press, 1988).

David Trotter, *Cinema and Modernism* (Oxford: Blackwell, 2007).

Gregory A. Waller (ed.), *Moviegoing in America* (Oxford and Malden, Mass.: Blackwell, 2002).

Robert Warshow, *The Immediate Experience* (Garden City, NY: Doubleday, 1962).

George Wilson, *Narration in Light* (Baltimore: Johns Hopkins University Press, 1986).

Peter Wollen, *Signs and Meaning* (London: BFI Publishing, 1979).

Peter Wollen, *Singin' in the Rain* (London: BFI Publishing, 1992).

Virginia Woolf, 'The Cinema', in *The Captain's Death-Bed and Other Essays* (New York and London: Harcourt Brace Jovanovich, 1978).

Around the world in 80 films

The following list is not arbitrary, since there is substantial agreement about the importance of these works. But it leaves out a large number of very good films, and I offer it to readers only as a set of suggestions, chances of exciting journeys in the world of cinema and the cinema of the world.

Argentina

Hour of the Furnaces (Getino/Solanas) 1973
The Swamp (Martel) 2001

Brazil

Antonio das Mortes (Glauber Rocha) 1969
Bus 174 (Padilha/Lacerda) 2002
Central Station (Salles) 1998
Land in Anguish (Glauber Rocha) 1967

China

Hero (Zhang) 2002
Still Life (Zhangke) 2006
Yellow Earth (Chen) 1984

Cuba

The Last Supper (Gutierrez Alea) 1976
Memories of Underdevelopment (Gutierrez Alea) 1968

Denmark

Breaking the Waves (von Trier) 1996
Day of Wrath (Dreyer) 1943

France

Breathless (Godard) 1960
Children of Paradise (Carné) 1945
La Jetée (Marker) 1962
Night and Fog (Resnais) 1955
Pickpocket (Bresson) 1959
Rules of the Game (Renoir) 1939

Germany

Aguirre Wrath of God (Herzog) 1972
The Cabinet of Dr Caligari (Wiene) 1919
M (Lang) 1931
Nosferatu (Murnau) 1922
Not Reconciled (Straub) 1965
Pandora's Box (Pabst) 1929
Wings of Desire (Wenders) 1987

Hong Kong

Heroes Shed No Tears (Woo) 1986
In the Mood for Love (Kar-wei) 2000

Hungary

Colonel Redl (Szabo) 1985
The Red and the White (Jancsó) 1981

India

Chandralekha (Vasan) 1948
Pather Panchali (Ray) 1955
Salaam Bombay (Nair) 1988

Iran

Close Up (Kiorastami) 1994
Crimson Gold (Panahi) 2003

Italy

The Battle of Algiers (Pontecorvo) 1966
L'Avventura (Antonioni) 1960

La Dolce Vita (Fellini) 1960
Rocco and His Brothers (Visconti) 1960
Rome Open City (Rossellini) 1945

Japan

The Hidden Fortress (Kurosawa) 1958
In the Realm of the Senses (Oshima) 1976
Seven Samurai (Kurosawa) 1954
Tokyo Story (Ozu) 1953
Ugetsu Monogatari (Mizoguchi) 1953

Mali

Yeelen (Cissé) 1987

Mexico

Amores Perros (González Iñárritu) 2000
Los Olvidados (Buñuel) 1950
Maria Candelaria (Fernandez) 1944

Poland

Ashes and Diamonds (Wajda) 1958
Bariera (Skolimowski) 1966

Portugal

Voyage to the Beginning of the World (Oliveira) 1997

Russia/USSR

Battleship Potemkin (Eisenstein) 1925
Come and See (Klimov) 1985
Ivan the Terrible (Eisenstein) 1944, 1958
Man with a Movie Camera (Vertov) 1929
Nostalgia (Tarkovsky) 1983

Senegal

Ceddo (Sembene) 1977
God of Thunder (Sembene) 1971

Spain

Land without Bread (Buñuel) 1933
Viridiana (Buñuel) 1961
Volver (Almodóvar) 2006

Sweden

Persona (Bergman) 1966
Wild Strawberries (Bergman) 1957

Taiwan

The Terrorizer (Yang) 1986

UK

Brief Encounter (Lean) 1945
Kind Hearts and Coronets (Hamer) 1949
Peeping Tom (Powell) 1960
The Third Man (Reed) 1949

USA

An American in Paris (Minnelli) 1951
The Gold Rush (Chaplin) 1925
Goodfellas (Scorsese) 1990
Intolerance (Griffith) 1916
Mulholland Drive (Lynch) 2001
Nashville (Altman) 1975
The Scarlet Empress (Sternberg) 1934
The Searchers (Ford) 1956
Some Like It Hot (Wilder) 1959
Touch of Evil (Welles) 1958

Index

The bold, italic page numbers refer to pictures in the text.